Profitable Promises

Essays on Women, Science and Health

Ruth Hubbard

Common Courage Press   Monroe, Maine

Copyright © Ruth Hubbard 1995
All rights reserved.
Cover design by Matt Wuerker
Author photo by Margaret Randall

Library of Congress Cataloging-in-Publication data
Hubbard, Ruth, 1924—
Profitable promises : essays on women, science and
health / Ruth Hubbard.
p. cm.
Includes index.
ISBN 1-56751-041-8 (cloth).
— ISBN 1-56751-040-x (pbk.)
1. Medical genetics—Social aspects.
2. Women—Health and hygene—Sociological aspects.
3. Science—Political aspects.
I. Title.
RA418.H83   1994
306.4'61—dc20   94-37839
CIP

Common Courage Press
P.O. Box 702
Monroe, ME 04951
207-525-0900 fax: 207-525-3068

First Printing

For Zeke

Contents

Part III
Toward a Political Understanding of Science

Acknowledgments, by Way of an Introduction

This collection would not exist but for the persistent, tactful prodding of Greg Bates and Flic Shooter of Common Courage Press. They suggested that I pull together some of my talks and articles of the last few years and did most of the work of turning them into a book. I am grateful for their labors and the graciousness and humor which have made our collaboration a pleasure.

I also want to thank the many colleagues and friends who stimulated me to produce the original manuscripts on which these essays are based and for inviting me to participate in their workshops, meetings, and publications. Beyond these specific stimuli, everything I have thought about and written in the past decade that touches on genetics, procreation, or health bears the imprint of my on-going collaboration with the members of the human genetics commitee, staff, and board members of the Council for Responsible Genetics (5 Upland Road, #3, Cambridge, MA 02140). By thinking and arguing about our own and each other's work, and writing together or critiquing each other's writings, we have engaged in collaborations that have been both supportive and critical. Since I have spent much of my recent professional life swimming against the scientific mainstream, people sometimes ask whether I have not felt lonely. The reason I haven't is, in large

7

measure, due to the fact that our small, but active, organization has generated a level of collectivity that has made me never lack for someone to help me to think through troubling issues or to find the right words to frame and discuss them. The responsibility for what appears on the printed page, of course, is mine, but much of the thinking has been done collectively.

Clearly, someone my age must also acknowledge years of help and support from family members and too many colleagues and friends to thank individually. Leaving them unnamed does not decrease my gratitude.

* * *

Most of the essays in this collection have been published, or are in the process of being published, elsewhere. Some also draw heavily on material Elijah Wald and I published in *Exploding the Gene Myth* (Beacon Press, 1993). However, I am such a compulsive editor of my own and other people's work that none of them is precisely as published in other places. With that proviso, these essays have been, or will soon be, published as follows: "Predictive Genetics and the Construction of the Healthy Ill" in the *Suffolk University Law Review*; "Transparent Women, Visible Genes and New Conceptions of Disease" in the *Cambridge Quarterly*; "Canceling a Conference on 'Genetics and Crime': Censorship or Scientific Responsibility?" in *Genewatch*; "Gay Genes?" as an op-ed article in the *New York Times*; "Women's Health: Some New Wrinkles on Some Old Issues" in the *Radcliffe Quarterly*; portions of "Sexism and Sociobiology: For

Acknowledgments

Our Own Good and the Good of the Species" originally in *Psychology Today*, and the entire article in *How Harvard Rules*, edited by Jack Trumpbour; "Which Facts? Whose Life? A Review of *The Facts of Life*" in *Nature;* "The Politics of Fetal/Maternal Conflict" in *Power and Decision: The Social Control of Reproduction*, edited by Gita Sen and Rachel C. Snow; "Of Genies and Bottles: Technology, Values and Choices" in "Women, Science and Technology: The Legacy of Margaret Benston" in *Canadian Woman Studies/Les cahiers de la femme;* "Constructs of Race Difference" is taken from "Constructs of Genetic Difference: Race and Sex," published in *Genes and Human Self-Knowledge: Historical and Philosophical Reflections on Modern Genetics*, edited by Robert F. Weir, Susan C. Lawrence, and Evan Fales, and published in a different version in *Challenging Racism and Sexism: Alternatives to Genetic Explanations (Genes and Gender VII)*, edited by Ethel Tobach and Betty Rosoff; "The Social Practice of Science: A Review of Donna Haraway's *Primate Visions*" in the *Village Voice;* "Science and Feminism: Comments on 'Building Two-Way Streets: The Case of Feminism and Science'" in *NWSA Journal;* and "In a Science Restructured Along Feminist Lines, Would the Laws of Gravity No Longer Hold?" in *Re-Visioning the Curriculum*, edited by Joyce Ladenson, Lisa Fine, and Kathleen Gessler.

Part I

The Link Between Genes, Illness and Behaviors

Introduction to Part I

This collection is based on recent articles and talks that build on my *The Politics of Women's Biology* (1990), and on *Exploding the Gene Myth* (1993) which I wrote with Elijah Wald. The essays in this section have grown out of my concern over the increasing extent to which our lives are being medicalized and geneticized. Even while we are in good health, and from before we are born until after we die, medical experts and laboratories are eager to sample us so as to try to foretell what diseases or disabilities we or our descendants may be heir to. Though this foreknowledge is advertised as enriching our lives, the real profits go to the scientific and technical entrepreneurs who pioneer and market the tests to which we are encouraged to submit.

In a television program aired by the British Broadcasting Corporation in June 1993, a medical expert warned that, unless everyone takes a particular new genetic test, some of us who show no signs of the condition whose presence this test supposedly detects might never know that we, in fact, have it. Though I hope the irony of this physician's statement does not escape you, she was being entirely serious. However, the television program also revealed that her research into this condition (called fragile X syndrome) was being supported, in part, by the very biotechnology company that markets the test kits used to detect the condition and that analyzes the test samples she collects. Such not so subtle conflicts of interest are becoming all too common.

As a result of the current genomania, our world

is being increasingly peopled by what are coming to be called the healthy, or asymptomatic, ill. While presymptomatic tests draw our attention away from the problems and joys of our daily lives, we try to foresee the manner and time of our eventual demise. It is as though we are not aware that a certain amount of illness and disability are inevitable and, instead of living our lives, we become preoccupied with investigating our likely alternatives for sickening and dying. Meanwhile, the medical-industrial complex fosters the illusion that its predictions are themselves equivalent to prevention.

This not only makes us needlessly dependent on medical and scientific experts whose views and forecasts often change quite radically from one day to the next. It also draws our attention away from the major problems that needlessly threaten the health of large segments of the world's population, such as hunger, malnutrition, urban squalor, and the old and new infections that flourish under these conditions. It would be far better to spend our preventive and health care resources on these prevalent, pressing problems than on the ones that may lurk in our genes.

It is sometimes convenient to dismiss appraisals and criticisms like these as opposing progress or as anti-science. But that is altogether too facile. Science is a useful way to learn about nature, including ourselves, and with proper guidance and supervision, its technological results can make life better. The problem is that, at present, the benefits science can bring us are overvalued, as compared with the benefits we could derive from other creations of the human imagination, be they cultural or political.

And when technology is harnessed to yield profits for the few rather than to improve the lives of most people, science and its technological products undermine rather than enhance our lives.

Geneticization distorts our priorities not only in the biomedical arena. Conservative psychologists and other social scientists are dusting off old arguments linking genes to poverty, intelligence, and "criminality." The *Boston Globe* (August 9, 1994) reports that Harvard psychologist Richard Herrnstein, who tried to link genes, intelligence, and social class in the early 1970s, has just co-authored a new book with Charles Murray, a fellow at the American Enterprise Institute and advocate of Dickensian measures such as putting "neglected children" into orphanages. The *Globe* quotes Herrnstein as saying that their book "establish[es] a link between intelligence and a whole range of societal behavior—economic success, criminal activity, welfare dependence and educational performance, for example." So, what else is new?

It is easy to establish such "links," though these generalizations are, in fact, shot through with exceptions and hence do not explain individual fates. What researchers need to find out is why these correlations exist. To assume that the answer is "genes," as Herrnstein and Murray do, just begs the question.

Even if it were possible to establish correlations between some genetic variations and social indicators, genetics will not explain the differences in the extent of poverty, illiteracy, drug addiction, and incarceration between the United States and Canada, just as genetics cannot explain the comparable differences in the incidence of AIDS. To explain such differences we must compare relevant social policies. In such comparisons, the United States does badly all across the board. But always, it is more convenient to attribute health conditions and social problems to the biological or psychological characteristics of individuals rather than to acknowledge and implement the changes needed to bring the living standards of large segments of the U.S. population to the level of those of our neighbor to the north.

"Good" Genes, "Bad" Genes

and the Imperialization of Human Experience

Ever since the concept of heredity was grafted onto molecules of DNA, scientists have endowed these molecules with a mythic potency. Increasingly, our notions about health and illness and about various forms of human behavior are being shaped by scientific knowledge of the way DNA functions. But these notions have a much longer history than our ideas about DNA have. It is important that we not fall prey to this imperializing of human experience by viewing all of it through the lens of genetics, which really is one of the narrowest foci to define our biology, not to mention what our social being is about.

This essay is concerned with predictive genetics, embryo selection, and germ-line gene manipulation, all of which involve much larger issues than the technical considerations. Abby Lippman, a genetic epidemiologist at McGill University, has coined the word "geneticization" to underline the fact that the genetic focus ignores the myriad of other biological, as well as social and economic and political, factors that contribute to shaping our lives, including our states of health and illness.

The attempt to use genes to explain people's medical conditions or social characteristics is based on the assumption that genes serve as the blue-prints for traits. We have learned to talk about genes "for" this or that trait. Thus, we are some-times told that eye color is transmitted through the genes and that it is inherited, and that there are genes "for" the pigment that give you brown eyes, and if you don't have those you get blue eyes. Essentially, eye color is presented in terms of brown or blue. But if you look in a mirror, or look at the people around you, almost nobody has what you would call blue eyes or brown eyes. They usually are intermediate in color, with flecks and varieties of hue and so on.

Traits that get described so simply (or the traits that get predicted so simply, as in "you've got it" or "haven't got it") seldom turn out to be that simple. There are always variations and the predictions can't tell us anything about them. This is true even for those relatively rare conditions that we have tra-ditionally thought of (traditionally being the last half-century or so) as genetic. Conditions such as cystic fibrosis, Huntington disease, sickle cell ane-mia—that is, conditions that children inherit from their parents in relatively predictable ways. Even with those predictions, we usually cannot foretell the extent of the disability or the age of its onset, and we have no way of judging ahead of time the quality of life of a person who has, or will have, the condition. In fact, of course, there is no way of pre-dicting anyone's quality of life, or to judge it for any-one other than oneself. And our judgments about ourselves often change over time.

Now, all of this is even truer of the much more common and complex conditions that appear to have some familial components—conditions such as diabetes, or high blood pressure, or cancer. Or the various behavioral characteristics that are being drawn into the genetic net that has begun to envelop us. For all of these, the predictions are relatively weak, and in many ways, they are largely irrelevant. Our lives do not follow a linear course from conception to death. Yet the emphasis on genes implies just that sort of linearity and predictability. Also, we are told, genetic predictions will give us useful information about ourselves. But the experience of most conditions is very different from our theoretical preconceptions about them.

Let us take cancer as an example. Cancer is truly a dread disease. Of what benefit would it be for me to know that I have a greater than usual susceptibility to, say, breast cancer, when I know full well that such a prediction does *not* mean that I will develop the cancer and that not having this prediction doesn't mean that I won't develop it?

Futhermore, breast cancer, or any serious condition, in the abstract and in anticipation, can be very different from the real experience of it. Two of my closest friends have died of breast cancer. I don't want to sentimentalize the issue, but I was struck by the fact that both of them insisted that the time since their diagnosis had been the most meaningful part of their lives. This may be a reflection of the terrible way in which we live our lives—that having that kind of thing laid on us forces us to make choices and arrange our priorities in ways that make our lives more meaningful than they were before. But I am using it to illustrate my point that predictive diagnoses convey the terror without being able to convey the substance of the experience. Yet, though this kind of foreknowledge is not particularly useful to us, it may indeed be useful to employers, insurers, and other forces in this society that can use the information to increase their profits or to discriminate against us and limit our lives in various ways.

The Politics of Prediction and Consent

Equally disturbing issues are coming up in the area of prenatal diagnosis. Within the next few years, when it becomes possible to isolate fetal cells from a pregnant woman's blood, physicians will be able to perform all kinds of tests without any of the more invasive prenatal diagnostic procedures that have to be done now.

But even now, predictive prenatal tests—of which so far only a few can be performed using blood samples—are being done without the woman's consent. This is rationalized by saying, "Why waste time by explaining complex conditions to a woman when it is very unlikely that any of them will be detected? Understanding the significance of the specific tests won't have any relevance to most of the women being tested. Better to do the tests and then explain their implications only to the women and families who need to become familiar with them." But of course that denies women the right to refuse to be tested. It completely circumvents the consent process, although, in theory, "informed consent" is required for any medical procedure. In fact, even now few pregnant women know—or know to ask—what tests will be done with the blood samples that are routinely drawn during prenatal visits.

"Informed consent" presumably protects both

consumers and providers of health care. The requirement was instituted in the 1970s to prevent the use of sick people to test drugs or medical procedures. An example of earlier practices that sent shock waves through the medical and civil rights communities was the infamous Tuskegee experiment in which uneducated African-American men who had syphilis were regularly examined over many years for what they were told was "bad blood," without having their infections treated. This was justified as necessary in order to document the "natural course" of their syphilis until they died. Presumably the requirement to inform patients of their diagnosis and treatment options would have prevented this abuse. "Informed consent" also protects providers against accusations by former patients that they performed procedures the patient would have refused had she or he understood the effects and consequences.

However, at present predictive genetic tests are proliferating at such a rate that in June 1994, a professor of medicine in Houston and a professor of law and public health in Boston published a joint article in the prestigious *New England Journal of Medicine* in which they argued that the situation is becoming too complex for most prospective parents to absorb all the information they would need to give truly informed consent for all the available tests. The authors therefore proposed that prospective parents be informed only sufficiently to understand the *principle* of genetic screening, and asked to give "generic consent" for their fetuses to undergo whatever tests are available. This proposal certainly simplifies the situation for providers and might work nicely for generic parents of generic future or present children. It hardly seems suited to meet the needs of the actual parents of a specific fetus or child.

In reality, a great many women, particularly in the medical system as it exists in the United States, don't have any idea about what their rights are and that they should have the right to consent. Underlying the notion that it's all right to perform tests without prior truly informed consent is the assumption that surely, if a test exists, everyone will want to have it. And that obviously stems from the kinds of class and cultural differences that exist between medical professionals and the vast mass of their clients.

Embryo Selection and the Genetic Ideology

I want to move on and say a few words about embryo selection, another technology which is becoming possible—it is certainly something that has been practiced with animals for a very long time. Once it is explored a little further, it could become attractive to people who would like to have "control" over the genetic predispositions of their children but feel uncomfortable about abortion. The in vitro fertilization procedure (IVF)—and from here on I will be building on the IVF procedure—routinely yields six or more embryos. Now, it is technically quite possible to allow these embryos to go through the first few cell divisions outside a woman's womb until each embryo contains six or eight cells. At that stage of embryonic development, all these cells are equivalent. It is therefore all right, as far as we know, to remove one of those cells. The remaining embryo—the whole embryo minus that one cell—

can then be frozen, while that one cell is tested to see if any problems can be predicted on the basis of chromosomal or genetic inspection. Then, if the embryo "passes the test," it can be thawed out and implanted and will develop just as it would have if it had not gone through this procedure.

This procedure gets around some of the thorny issues with therapeutic abortions partway through an already started pregnancy, since most people don't feel about an embryo conceived in vitro the way they feel about an embryo that has begun to develop in a woman's uterus. But of course this entire procedure, from beginning to end, is based on an enormously abstract way of looking at health, disease, and human characteristics. It seems like science fiction to be told that these four embryos are "better" than these other two and why not pick "the best" of the lot. I suspect that it does not involve a great deal of emotion for the prospective parents though, of course, it requires a good deal of money. So, in fact, this procedure could become quite acceptable among people who can afford it.

I am very concerned about this scenario because the judgments that can be made on this basis are quite meaningless since, as I said before, most inherited conditions are highly variable, and depend on many factors other than those the tests can detect. So, in fact, people are encouraged to act as though they know what they are doing when they are just blindly following a genetic ideology with little real meaning. How embryos develop into fetuses, and fetuses into babies, and babies into children, and children into adults depends on a myriad of unpredictables. In addition, I am troubled by the whole business of sorting "good" and "bad" traits. Who is to say which of us is "good enough" to be born?

Forces Driving the Fertility Industry

So why focus on genes and genetic predictions in embryos? I think that one answer is that for biologists, this is very fascinating science. There was no way to do human embryology until Drs. Patrick Steptoe and Robert Edwards, the British "scientific parents" of Louise Brown (the first child to be born as a result of IVF) were able to persuade women that IVF is to their benefit. And while it can, indeed, be to some families' benefit, we have to recognize that a host of exciting science has become possible by virtue of getting people to accept IVF as desirable in their own lives.

Also, the use of these procedures is making some people rich. Many fertility clinics and in vitro clinics operate for profit. And even though many of these clinics have few positive results (meaning, babies) to show, since the U.S. fertility industry is largely unregulated, it has become one of the exciting and lucrative places to be, financially.

Somatic and Germline Manipulation

Let me now move on and say a word about genetic manipulation. This is usually referred to as gene therapy but I purposely avoid that term because "therapy" implies benefits. The term is used instead of "treatment" or "experimentation" for its PR value.

Genetic manipulation comes in two forms. One,

called "somatic gene therapy" (or somatic genetic manipulation), is now in the experimental stages. It involves inserting genes into differentiated tissues (that is, into lung tissue, or blood-forming cells, or other specialized tissues) of a person who has a particular condition that scientists are trying to remedy through this manipulation. Such scientists are trying to replace genes that are not functioning the way they should be in a particular tissue with genes that, they hope, will function better. There are a number of protocols like that being followed, and some of them seem to be fulfilling the promise of improving the condition in question. To my way of thinking, this is not very different from any other form of high tech therapy. It is expensive, and therefore not accessible to everybody who should get it, but it can be stopped, or changed, if it looks like it is not working the way it was meant to work.

There is another form of gene manipulation that is so far only a potential—but a very real potential. And if you follow the literature, as I have done, you will notice that some of the people involved in somatic gene manipulation are changing the way they talk about it. A few years ago they were saying, "Well, of course we are only going to do somatic manipulation, we are never going to do germ-line manipulation." (I'll explain that term in a moment.) Today they are saying, "You know, germ-line and somatic manipulaton are not that different and if we cannot achieve what we want by the use of somatic cell manipulation, there's really no reason why we shouldn't try germ-line." ("Somatic cells" is what biologists call all cells in the body except sperm or eggs. These latter are called "germ cells.")

Here is what "germ-line manipulation" means, and why it is a problem. You start with IVF and let the fertilized egg develop into an early embryo, and you test one cell from this embryo, as I have described before. Then, if you find that you want to make a genetic alteration, you make the alteration in that embryo: you insert the genetic material you want in there into one or more of the cells of this early embryo. Once you do that, this genetic material will presumably become incorporated into the individual into which this embryo will develop. It will get into most, or possibly all, of that person's cells, including their germ cells, that is, their eggs or sperm, depending on whether they are female or male. A manipulation of the germ-line, therefore, means a permanent change not only in the person into whom the embryo develops, but in their genetic line: It involves a change in a future person and that person's future offspring.

That, in principle, is a very different kettle of fish from somatic manipulations, which are designed to alter an existing condition in an actual person. For one thing, we have to recognize that we are not, in fact, benefitting someone who is now with us and who has some disease. We are presumably benefitting someone who may get born and who, we are afraid, will have some condition if we do not interfere in this way.

But if people are desperate not to have a child with a potential genetic prediction which runs in their family and want to avoid the possibility of abortion, this can be done by means of embryo selection. You don't really need to do germ-line intervention. In only extremely rare circumstances would that not be the case, and surely for those rare situations other things are possible, such as donor insemination, or egg donation, if not adoption. It does not make sense to initiate a procedure that casts its shadow over future generations to solve virtually non-existent health problems.

If we don't actually need germline manipulation, why is it being talked about? Discussions of germ-line interventions are increasingly centered on so-called "enhancement" therapies. That is, people are not just talking about trying to prevent some dire medical condition, but to create "enhanced" human beings. What if it becomes possible to predict intelligence (I'm not saying this is possible, only putting it forth because it is an example that is often used) and other "desirable" social traits? Wouldn't it be nice if we could improve on the population by manipulating early embryos? This is a particularly weird form of eugenics—making decisions about what future people are the right kinds of people to have around and what are the wrong kinds of people.

In case you think this is just fantasy, consider the opinion of Daniel Koshland, a molecular biologist and editor of *Science*, the most prestigious science weekly in the country, in which he writes editorials quite frequently. In one of these editorials, he was discussing the desirability of germ-line genetic manipulations, and saying, "If a child destined to have a permanently low IQ could be cured [note the word] by replacing a gene, would anyone really argue against that?" And he goes on to say, "It's a short step from that decision to improving a normal IQ. Is there an argument against making superior individuals? Not superior morally and not superior philosophically, just superior in certain skills—better at computers, better musicians, better physically? As society gets more complex, perhaps it must select for individuals more capable of coping with its complex problems."

This kind of argument, again, relies excessively on genes as the source of human excellence. It also implies that we know what constitutes "excellence," what traits had best be enhanced, and which should be eliminated or suppressed. Yet, we have no proper societal guidelines for making these decisions. Is there any individual or group you would trust to make such choices?

Leroy Walters, a bioethicist at Georgetown University, stated in a talk about germ-line genetic therapy that he feels it is inevitable and that we should welcome it. He used as an example that he wished he didn't need as much sleep as he does. He hates to be wasting all this time sleeping and wouldn't it be nice to do germ-line manipulation so that people wouldn't have to sleep so much? Is that a good reason to develop an expensive and intrinsically worrisome technology?

In a way, most troubling about all this is not just the trivial, but dangerous, level to which this is moving. You may have read in the papers that the March of Dimes commissioned a poll that indicated that many people are relatively sanguine about all forms of genetic manipulation, including this so-called enhancement therapy. But when these same people were asked whether they think they know enough about genetics to make such decisions, some 80% said they do not. People are getting onto

28

a bandwagon, though they are perfectly willing to admit that they haven't the least idea of what is in fact going on.

It is important to recognize that these technological innovations will involve dangers to come. But, in a way, the technical dangers are the least of it. The ideological and political dangers of overvaluing biological inheritance, and of making decisions about good and bad genes, and good and bad characteristics, are far greater. It is said that the road to hell is paved with good intentions. I'm not sure that the intentions involved here are so great, but the road surely will lead to a hell if we use grounds that have no validity to make decisions we shouldn't be making about the relative value of different human lives.

Predictive Genetics

and the Construction of the Healthy Ill

> It seems to be forgotten both that science and technology have had endless failures, and that their successes have always depended on concentrating on the things that work and avoiding what does not. In designing 'futures', a few mildly hopeful existing omens are extrapolated without limit. With hardly anything presently in the bank, blank checks are drawn on behalf of chosen techniques—a process which continues long after their limitations have become obvious.
>
> Mary Midgley, *Science as Salvation: a Modern Myth and its Meaning.*[1]

Definitions of Health and Illness

I'd like to assess some of the problems likely to result from the new technologies that enable medical practitioners to offer genetic predictions about future health conditions. But before doing that, we need to take a critical look at what we mean by heath and illness.

Our culture tends to regard these as biological phenomena, but our health is not simply a matter of biology. A range of social, economic, and biological circumstances affect our body states and our sense

31

of health and well being, and also shape the ways we perceive, define, and categorize them. Most of the time, biology cannot be sorted out from social and economic realities, because they build on each other and become so intertwined as to be inextricable. When we pretend that we can examine the biological factors in isolation, we oversimplify and distort the situation.

The categories of health and illness describe a continuum of experiences. At one end we feel in top form, at the other we feel terrible, and there are many gradations in between. Much of the time, the way we feel can fluctuate from one moment to the next depending on what else is happening in our lives. At what point along that continuum we decide we are sick, at what point we decide we need advice, and to whom we go to get it depend on cultural practices, professionalization, and the costs of medical and other forms of assistance.

If we consult a physician or other health care provider, we run into a phenomenon that is typical of our medical culture: there is often a difference between the way we feel and the label that gets attached to us, our "diagnosis." Modern scientific medicine generalizes individual people's feelings and fits them into ready-made diagnostic categories. To this end, diseases are delineated as discrete entities as though they had an existence of their own. The physician's or nurse practitioner's task then is to search for the signs and symptoms that identify what disease a given person "has." This way of looking at things encourages scientists to search for specific, definable causes and cures without raising questions about how people's health conditions are related to, and fit into, the circumstances of their lives.

The modern notion that symptoms are not body states or feelings experienced by specific individuals, but that they can be subsumed in diseases with their own names and characteristics, as though they had an existence apart from the people who experience them, evoked vigorous debates well into the nineteenth century. Characters in the novels of turn-of-the-century authors, such as Tolstoy and Rilke, complained that the new, scientific medicine was severing their existential relationships to their diseases and thus to themselves. Tolstoy's Ivan Ilych complained that the way he felt was of no interest to his physician, who cared only about the state of his kidneys.[2] Rilke's Malte Laurids Brigge railed at hospitals that make it impossible for people to experience the agony of their own personal death.[3]

The idea that diseases are discrete, diagnosable entities initially elicited opposition within the profession as well, but it is now part of our medical and scientific culture. Though we complain when we take feelings of malaise to the doctor and are told that "nothing is wrong," we accept the verdict. Similarly, we have learned to consult medical practitioners for regular so-called check-ups, even when we feel fine. At such times we are basically asking them to give us permission to go on feeling all right. Whether we are diagnosed as healthy or ill, we tend to assign greater value to this judgment than to our own sense of well-being. In fact, sometimes a verdict that "nothing is wrong" makes us feel better than we did before and a diagnosis of a definable—or ill-defined—health problem can make us feel bad even though nothing else has changed.

I will never forget the wife of a colleague who had died following surgery for a recently diagnosed cancer. While relating the story of her husband's unexpected death, she said, with evident approval of the medical intervention: "We would not even have known he had cancer, if he had not gone for a routine check-up." She was so sure that he had done the right thing in having this "routine check-up" that she apparently overlooked the fact that his death was a consequence of the medical intervention and not of the cancer.

While I am not suggesting that we should never consult a practitioner, I am not sure it makes sense to do so when we are feeling fine, just on the chance that he or she might detect a serious condition in its early, asymptomatic stages. At the very least, we should think about this question and not blindly follow our present medical culture, which puts excessive reliance on the benefits of early detection and prediction.

The idea that diseases are well-defined, diagnosable entities was reinforced when bacteria and viruses began to be thought of as causing specific conditions. And it is true that the identification of these transmissible agents has made it possible to develop public health and medical measures to minimize or prevent the occurrence of some infectious diseases and to treat them with antibacterial or antiviral drugs or vaccines. However, the relationship of infectious agents to disease is far from simple and its current interpretation involves many political assumptions.[4]

Predictive Genetics

Contrary to what we usually hear, in the industrialized world mortality rates from almost all known infectious diseases were already decreasing for many decades *before* the offending bacterial or viral agents were identified. And deaths from such infections as smallpox, tuberculosis, scarlet fever, measles, and whooping cough were on the decline long before the vaccines or drugs that are effective against them were developed.[5] Thomas McKeown, a British population scientist, attributes their decline to innovations in agriculture and transportation, which increased the availability of a greater variety of foods and so improved nutrition, and to sanitary measures that provided more healthful water and better sewage disposal and housing. In the poor countries of the so-called Third World most of these scourges have not been eliminated precisely because diagnoses, drugs, and vaccines, as such, are not enough to counteract the health-undermining effects of poverty and the lack of adequate public health measures.

Even in the industrialized world, access to health care in itself does not make people healthy. Data collected in Great Britain in the 1970s (even before Conservative governments began to dismantle the National Health Service) show that, while twenty-five years of universal access to free health care had improved people's health (indeed beyond what has been achieved in the United States), mortality rates were still inversely correlated with social class: the lower a family's social class, the higher was the mortality rate of both women and men of that class. This was equally true for deaths from treatable infectious diseases, from chronic conditions such as cancer or diseases of the circulatory or digestive system, and from obviously social causes, such as accidents, poisoning, or violence.[6]

In the United States, we are now seeing a recurrence of epidemics of several major infectious diseases that we thought were long gone, or at least under control, such as tuberculosis, measles, syphilis, and gonorrhea.[7] Many of these epidemics can be traced to specific social factors, such as homelessness, overcrowding, and a lack of funds for vaccinations and other public health measures, as well as to the absence of a coherent program to stem the spread of sexually transmitted diseases and HIV infection.

Biomedical researchers tend to concentrate on problem solving, rather than on ways to make existing solutions accessible. This may be a reasonable strategy for a research scientist, but in our society, with its exaggerated confidence in technical solutions, scientists' promises that they can solve our health problems focus too much attention on germs or, currently, on genes, and draw it away from more basic societal influences. In doing so, biomedical scientists ensure their monopoly over funding for disease-prevention by concentrating it in scientific institutes and laboratories. Broader political analyses of the incidence of disease, based on class and ethnicity, are given short shrift in professional and public discussions of how best to prevent disease and enhance health.

Health and disease become defined as scientific problems for which we must seek scientific answers. Health becomes a technical problem, rather than a social problem that requires social and economic remedies at least as much as scientific and medical ones. With the advent of genetic diagnoses, biomedical scientists now promise to reveal—and overcome—the mysteries involved in chronic conditions, such as cancer, heart diseases, diabetes, or Alzheimer disease and also in stigmatized behaviors, such as homosexuality, alcoholism, or violence.

Genes as Predictors of Health and Disease

Long before the recent focus on genes, medical practitioners have tended to begin their assessment of our state of health by asking us about our "family history"—the diseases members of our family have had. Only later, if at all, are we likely to be asked about our lives: where we live, what range of foods we eat, or how we feel about our domestic and other relationships. Unless our complaints are directly work-related, we are rarely asked about where we work or the nature of our job, even though many people are exposed to health hazards at their place of work.

Delineating a "family history" represents an attempt to come up with a genetic framework into which our problems can be fitted. Health practitioners then use this information about our relatives' health conditions to help them assess what we may expect in our own lives. Such histories can include only what we happen to know or remember about our family and therefore give only a rough picture. Modern genetic diagnoses try to go beyond that by looking at specific biological manifestations of inherited traits and eventually at so-called genetic markers or genes themselves.

Before we examine more closely the kinds of

information the new technologies can reveal, we need to clarify what genes are and how they function. This is important because the predictive significance of genetic information is often exaggerated or misstated.

Genes are specific, functional segments of the DNA molecules that lie along the length of each of our twenty-three pairs of chromosomes. These segments, or genes, come in different sizes, and are part of the metabolic apparatus of cells and organisms. Their function is to specify the linear sequence of the building blocks of the proteins. (These building blocks are called amino acids.) Some genes also specify the rate at which proteins are synthesized. Genes are important because different proteins are involved in all aspects of our bodily functions, and the composition of each kind of protein is specified by a particular gene. Hemoglobin, the red pigment in our blood that transports oxygen from the lungs to the tissues, is a protein. Our hair and fingernails are proteins. Large portions of our muscles and tendons are proteins. Enzymes and antibodies are proteins. Some hormones are proteins. In a word, proteins participate in just about everything that goes on in our bodies and this is what makes both them and genes important. However, just because proteins play such important and varied roles and because many of them participate in a wide range of metabolic functions, it is virtually impossible to specify the effects any one protein, or gene, will exert at any given time, much less over a life-time.

This means that, although the function of a specific DNA segment (or gene) may be predictable in the narrow sense that we can say that it specifies the composition of this or that protein, we cannot predict the potential range or significance of its effects. For this reason, it is wrong to say that genes "cause," "control," or "program" a specific trait or that they are "blueprints" of organisms or of life. They are simply some among the many chemical compounds that participate in the intricate networks of reactions that go on in organisms.

We are *not* the expression of our genes, and knowing their location on the chromosomes, or their composition, does not enable someone to predict what we will look or be like. We are the expression of everything that goes on inside and around us from the moment each one of us was conceived, or even before. If either or both our parents were poorly nourished, drank too much alcohol or smoked, were exposed to toxic chemicals or radiation at work or where they were living, that may affect who we are. Sometimes it may do so by altering our genes, but more usually by affecting some other aspect of our metabolism. Indeed, it may prevent our developing properly or being born altogether. Of course, once we are born, lots of things in our environment can affect the way we develop and grow, as well as our health. It is a mistake to put too much weight on genes or DNA.

At present, when scientists try to make genetic predictions, they often look at what they call "markers"—short pieces of DNA, which, they think, lie near the particular gene that interests them. In a few rare instances, they can isolate and examine the gene itself. As the Human Genome Project—the effort to catalog and analyze all of our genes—unfolds, the rate at which scientists are identifying and localizing different markers and genes is increasing all the time.

Once scientists can localize sets of markers or a gene associated with a specific trait, they can begin to identify alterations or variations in the gene. Such variations are called "mutations" and the different variants of a gene are called its "alleles."

When scientists identify a mutation in a gene that participates in the synthesis of a critical enzyme, because the mutation interferes with the function that enzyme ordinarily performs, it often becomes relatively easy for them to develop a genetic test for the condition associated with the malfunction. Thus, we now have tests for variants (alleles) of the genes implicated in cystic fibrosis, sickle cell anemia, phenylketonuria (PKU), Tay Sachs disease, Huntington disease, and other conditions whose patterns of inheritance within families are fairly predictable because they follow the statistical laws described by the Czech monk Gregor Mendel over a century ago.

Such tests are not intended for people who know they have one of these conditions because they experience its symptoms. But they can be used to predict the condition in fetuses. They can also be used to identify people who have not yet developed symptoms of late-onset conditions, such as Huntington disease and some forms of muscular dystrophy. Predictive tests also make it possible for people to learn that they carry one gene with a mutation, where the condition would only become evident if they had two copies of that same allele. (Following Mendel's original nomenclature, such alleles, and the corresponding conditions, are called "recessive.") This fact could be of interest in the context of procreation, since if someone happened to carry the same allele as her or his partner did, each of their children would have one chance in four of inheriting that allele from both parents, in which case the child would be likely to manifest the condition in question.

The problem with such predictions is that, for most so-called genetic conditions, the severity of the symptoms can vary a good deal, both from person to person and for the same person over time. This can be so because other biochemical or environmental factors in addition to the specific inherited change in DNA may affect the manifestations of that condition. Also, different alleles of the same gene can lead to different outcomes. A predictive diagnosis, or name, attached to a future genetic condition usually cannot take the effects of such variables into account.

There is another, less technical problem with all forms of predictive diagnosis, whether or not they implicate genes. When such diagnoses are used to characterize the future health of a fetus, they contain very little information about what kind of a person that fetus will become and what significance the condition in question will have in her or his life or in the lives of the people among whom she or he will live.

However real a fetus may be to the woman whose body sustains it and to the rest of its future family, until it is born, it is a creature of their imagination. If a diagnosis of a potential health problem gets attached to it, this label is likely to dominate the way the family envisages this future person and overwhelm their plans and hopes. Once someone has been born, or has lived for a time, families tend to integrate that person's present or future health conditions with the rest of their feelings about her or him. At that point, parents often find that they are able to accept even a relatively serious health problem as a normal part of the life of that family because it just becomes part of who that family member is.

As increasing numbers of people must make decisions about whether to have prenatal tests and what to do about the results, research is showing that factors such as race, ethnicity, and class have a good deal to do with the way people relate to the availability of tests and also to the way they interpret and use the information the tests offer.[8,9] This is not surprising. Ideas about what constitutes a disability differ, and so do attitudes toward it as well as toward childbearing, pregnancy, and abortion.

In general, upper-class parents or parents who are professionals tend to be stricter in their requirements for what constitutes an acceptable fetus than other parents are. Anthropologist Rayna Rapp quotes statements by three families. Two of the families decided to terminate a pregnancy when their son was predicted to be born with a rare chromosomal condition (XXY, or Klinefelter syndrome) which tends to result in relatively poor development of the genitals and low fertility. Rapp writes: "One professional couple told [the genetic counselor], 'If he can't grow up to have a shot at becoming the president, we don't want him.'" (This sounds extreme, but may be so only in its frankness. Incidentally, this couple seems to have forgotten that Franklin D. Roosevelt, one of our greatest and most popular presidents, was severely disabled.) Rapp continues:

A low-income family said of the same condition, "A baby will have to face so many problems in this world, it isn't fair to add this one to the burdens he'll have." And a Puerto Rican single mother who chose to continue a pregnancy after getting a prenatal diagnosis of Klinefelter's said of her now four-year old son, "He's normal, he's growing up normal. As long as there is nothing wrong that shows, he isn't blind or deaf or crippled, he's normal as far as I'm concerned."[10]

Rapp reminds us that from the perspective of parents-to-be all predictive diagnoses are ambiguous, since they cannot foretell the degree of a future disability. How families integrate the information into their lives and how they act on it depends on variables that lie outside the range of their transactions with the professionals who perform the tests or interpret the results. The more profound the differences between the professionals and the families they test or counsel are in terms of language, education, class, or race/ethnicity, the less certain it becomes what messages prospective parents take with them, and how they interpret these messages and act on them. Even a word like "retarded," which may seem unambiguous to physicians or counselors, is laden with cultural meanings. "What is this retarded?" Rapp quotes a Haitian father. "They always say that Haitian children are retarded in the public schools. But when we put them in the Haitian Academy [a community-based private school], they do just fine." To this father chromosomes offer a "weak and abstract explanation for the problems a Haitian child may face."[11]

Another thing is becoming apparent: The more information future parents have about a potential disability, the less likely they may be to want a fetus tested or to terminate a pregnancy.[12,13] For example, people who know little about cystic fibrosis tend to be interested in predictive and prenatal tests and to think they would want to terminate a pregnancy if the fetus were predicted to be born with this condition. People who have a child with cystic fibrosis may decide not to have any more biological children or to have a prenatal test but, based on interviews conducted by sociologist Dorothy Wertz and her colleagues, most of them would not consider terminating a pregnancy if the next child were predicted to have cystic fibrosis. The reason, in part, is that therapies are improving and parents expect their future children to survive at least into mid-life. The data Wertz and her colleagues have collected show that, unless there is a prediction of "severe mental retardation" or of a condition expected to result in "death before age 5," only a minority of parents who have experience with cystic fibrosis would consider aborting a fetus because it is expected to develop such a condition.[14] Among other things, parents who have experience with raising a child with a disability realize that most conditions are too variable to permit an accurate prediction of their severity.

Usually, termination is the only available alternative to completing a pregnancy if a child has been predicted to be born with a condition for which prenatal tests are available. But some future parents prefer to know the prediction even though they expect to continue the pregnancy. Others want it in order to have the option to abort. I believe that every woman must have the right to terminate a pregnancy, no matter what her reasons may be. But from an ethical and political point of view, it is one thing to decide that one cannot, or does not want to, have a child at this time. It is another to want to have a child, but not the one into which this fetus is predicted to develop.

Most people in our society feel judgmental about future parents who base the decision to terminate a pregnancy on the fact that the fetus is of the "wrong" sex, but have sympathy with that decision when it involves a predicted disability. We need to look carefully at the basis on which we make this distinction. Is it really any easier for a woman in India to give birth to a girl, when she knows that this will make her and her daughter suffer for life, than it is for a U.S. family to accept raising a child with Down syndrome? Both kinds of decisions are embedded in societal barriers and prejudices which it would be best to challenge before we fall into the trap of believing that our children can be "made to order."

Predictive labeling always involves prejudgments and prejudices. In retrospect most people would admit that the world would not have been a better place without Woody Guthrie or Stephen Hawking, even though Guthrie had Huntington disease and Hawking has amyotrophic lateral sclerosis. And it would not be better without the people I know who are blind or deaf or have spina bifida, osteogenesis imperfecta, or some other disability. All of them contribute to society and are who they are both because, and in spite, of their health conditions. Who can say that they would be more complete and effective human beings without these health conditions? No one has the foreknowledge to decide who should or should not be part of the range of human diversity, and we do not want genetic commissars to deliver judgments about "who should and who should not inhabit the world."[15]

This is true of all those relatively rare conditions the probabilities of whose incidence can be predicted by the laws of Mendelian genetics, such as the ones I have been discussing so far. It is equally true for the much more prevalent and complex conditions one or another of which all of us are likely to experience some time before we die: diabetes, high blood pressure, cancer, Alzheimer disease, or one or another behavioral disorder, such as alcoholism, schizophrenia, or bipolar manic depression. All these involve the interplay of many factors, some of which may be inherited in some instances.

When these conditions run in families, we may suspect that they are being passed on biologically rather than by virtue of the fact that members of the same family usually have a good deal more than genes in common. But for any specific person their incidence can never be predicted with certainty. Yet, day by day scientists are identifying genes or "genetic markers" which they claim are associated with one or another of these common conditions. Even when scientists identify such markers or genes, it is clear that no single mutation is likely to account for any of these complex conditions. To the extent that genes are involved, there is always an interplay between numbers of genetic and environmental factors.

Nonetheless, scientific publications and reports in the media routinely cite statistical probabilities that someone who carries a newly discovered mutation will develop an associated condition. A recent example is the "gene for Alzheimer's" announced in the August 13, 1993 issue of *Science*, the prestigious weekly publication of the American Association for the Advancement of Science.[16] The article reports that members of families in which late-onset Alzheimer disease is common, but who *do not* carry the mutation described in this paper, have a 20 per cent likelihood of developing the condition by age 75. Among family members who have one copy of the mutated gene the incidence increases to 45 percent, and among those with two copies to 90 percent. Furthermore, the average age of onset tends to decrease from 84 years to 75 and 68 years, depending on the whether the family member has no, one, or two copies of the allele in question. The emphasis on "the gene for Alzheimer's" obscures the fact that these results equally show that having one or both altered alleles does not mean that one will necessarily develop the condition, nor does the absence of this allele mean that one will *not* develop Alzheimer disease.

As the commentary published in the same issue of *Science* points out, it might be useful for people to know these probabilities if there were something they could do to keep from developing Alzheimer disease, or to treat it when the early signs begin to appear.[17] Given that there isn't, this information is useless, irrespective of whether people have reason to think they may be at risk for the condition.

A recent Associated Press release announced a novel combination of psychological tests to "predict Alzheimer's." Though this procedure is not good at predicting who will develop the condition, it is supposedly better at guessing who will not. A quote from one of the authors of the published report illustrates the absurdity of such predictions. "If you score well on these tests," he reportedly said, "we can *confidently* say that over the next four years you *probably* won't be getting dementia (my italics).[18] Is it really worth doing research to achieve that level of information? And genetic predictions for complex conditions can offer no greater certainty.

Scientists counter these kinds of criticisms by saying that, though identifying a mutation is of no direct help, knowing its nature will make it easier to understand the corresponding changes in the protein the gene specifies. This, they say, will make it easier to figure out the biological mechanisms underlying the condition's overt manifestations.

History does not offer grounds for their optimism. For some twenty-five years, scientists have known the precise alteration in the hemoglobin molecule that underlies sickle cell anemia. They also know the precise location and nature of the mutation in the relevant DNA (or gene). Yet, this knowledge has not facilitated the development of therapies or cures for sickle cell anemia. The converse is true for PKU. Here an effective therapy to forestall the adverse effects of the mutation was developed decades before anyone could specify the location or identity of the relevant genetic mutation.

Both these examples involve well-characterized conditions whose patterns of inheritance follow Mendel's laws and whose incidence is relatively predictable. It is unlikely that complex conditions such as Alzheimer disease or breast or colon cancer will be open to therapeutic interventions once their incidence can be statistically correlated with alterations in one or another DNA sequence.

As with Alzheimer disease, predictive genetic tests for cancer have only statistical validity and hence are problematic. Despite this, DNA markers that can be correlated with the incidence of breast cancer or colon cancer in families, in which several family members have developed these cancers at relatively young ages, have received a good deal of publicity. Even within such "cancer-prone" families, the fact that someone tests positive for the relevant marker (or the allele, once it has been identified) does not mean that that person will definitely develop the cancer. Conversely, since most people who develop breast or colon cancer have no family history of these conditions, the fact that a family member does not have the marker (or allele) does not mean she or he won't develop the cancer. Scientists project that, once they identify the alleles they believe to be associated with these cancers in cancer-prone families, they will be able to develop predictive tests that can be used for population-wide screening. Yet, cancer—like Alzheimer disease—usually does not develop until late in life. Therefore, there will be no way to gauge the accuracy of these predictions until statistically significant numbers of people who have taken the test live out their entire lives. In the mean time, what are people to do who test positive for a putative "Alzheimer gene" or "cancer gene"?

Despite the fact that such predictions will express only probabilities, and not a certainty, that a specific person will, or will not, develop the condition in question, all such correlations can be used to yield predictive tests. Hence, there is a good deal of pressure from the scientific community and the biotechnology and pharmaceutical industries to develop predictive tests on the basis of our present, preliminary information. The reasons are largely economic. Most scientists working in this area have links to industry. For years they have promised more than the industry has delivered by way of useful therapies or cures.[19] Once a genetic marker or gene is identified, the industry can make good on its financial promises by developing predictive tests for any condition that is supposedly associated with a specific piece of DNA. From an economic perspective, predictive tests are much more profitable than therapies, since therapies are of use only to people who have the condition that the therapy is intended to improve or cure, whereas entire populations can be turned into consumers of predictive or screening tests.

Societal Implications of Genetic Labeling

Projects have been under way in Colorado and Georgia to administer a genetic test to children attending special education classes in the public schools to detect a condition called fragile X syndrome. The children are selected for testing on the basis of easily measured physical signs, such as the shape of their heads and size of their ears, which are thought to be characteristic of this condition.

Both the prevalence of the condition and the accuracy and predictive value of the test remain to be established. What is clear already is that some people who are identified as carrying the relevant mutation exhibit no detectable symptoms whereas others have signs of severe autism or mental retardation. And some people's symptoms fall along the entire spectrum between those extremes. In both Colorado and Georgia, testing requires parental consent and is therefore voluntary. Teachers supposedly are not told the results, though in Colorado they know which children are singled out for testing. It is hard to foresee precisely what, if any, beneficial effects this project will have for the parents, teachers, or children.

The research in Colorado is being supported by Oncor, Inc., a biotechnology company in Gaithersburg, Maryland, which produces the test kits and runs the tests for this project. In a television program aired by the British Broadcasting Company on June 7, 1993 on their PANORAMA program, David Bruning, identified as Genetics Marketing Manager at Oncor, suggests that eventually this test could be used not only to screen children suspected of having fragile X syndrome, but for population-wide testing in the United States, Great Britain, and the European continent in order to identify carriers of the mutation who evidence no symptoms. Without question this is good business, but it is not good medical, educational, or social policy.[20]

To look at health and illness through the lens of genetics distorts our priorities by drawing attention away from the many biological, psychological, social, and economic factors that affect our health and play a part in generating disease or preventing its development. A bad marriage, a stressful job, racial or sexual harassment and violence, and economic hardships all can stress our immune system, affect what and how much we eat and how we metabolize it, whether we smoke, drink, or use drugs, and whether we get a chance to relax or exercise. All these factors—and more—can influence whether we develop cancer, high blood pressure, heart disease, diabetes, arthritis, manic depression, and other chronic health conditions.

Looking at our genes does not help to change these circumstances and may make things worse by making us fatalistic about our future health. Furthermore, genetic predictions of ill health create a new class of "patients" who are coming to be referred to as the asymptomatic or healthy ill: people who have no symptoms, but are predicted to develop them at some undefined time in the future.

This kind of geneticization not only debilitates people by needlessly increasing our dependence on the scientific and medical professions, but it may get in the way of our family relationships and of our obtaining an education, a job, or health insurance. Genetic predictions reach beyond the individual who has been tested to her or his biological relatives, marriage partners, and present or future children and grandchildren. If one member of a biological family decides to be tested and tests positive, that implicates other members, some of whom may not want to know about their potential risk status or be tested. If genetic markers turn out not to be informative unless many family members are tested, the fact that some members want to know their risks puts pressure on the others to get tested. Genetic testing also can uncover family secrets about paternity or adoption.

The extent of potential ethical and practical conflicts has not been thought through, although it clearly is considerable. All the while, tests are being churned out at an increasing rate.

At this time, considerable thought is beginning to be given to the potential for genetic discrimination in education, employment, and insurance.[21,22,23,24,25]

One of the questions that needs to be sorted out is to what extent current legislation protects people against discrimination if they are not, in fact, disabled but are predicted to become so at some unpredictable time in the future. A "Task Force on Genetic Information and Insurance," formed by the Joint National Institutes of Health-Department of Energy Working Group on the Ethical, Legal, and Social Implications of Human Genome Research (ELSI), which operates under the auspices of the Human Genome Project, has recently issued its recommendations.[26] They encompass an admirable wish list, but give no practical guidelines for implementation.

With regard to the protection of privacy of genetic information in the civic or judicial arenas, legislation is at best spotty and mostly non-existent,[27,28] while genetic tests are being ground out faster than legislative and legal mechanisms can be put in place that adequately protect people.

Legislators, lawyers, and ordinary citizens need to begin now to counteract the deleterious consequence this technology and the ideology it fosters are bound to have on our social structures and relationships—from our interactions with our families and friends to our contacts with physicians, teachers, employers, insurers, or law enforcement agencies. We cannot afford to ignore the fact that we live in a time when the crudest of eugenic policies, including rape, are once more being advocated in Europe, this time by Serbs, people who (like the Germans before 1933) had been thought of as cultured and enlightened.

Technology is never neutral, least of all a technology that lures us with promises of enhancing our understanding of "what makes us human."[29]

Transparent Women, Visible Genes and New Conceptions of Disease

Until not so long ago, what went on inside a woman's body as she gestated her future babies had to be guessed at—by her and by the people on whom she called to assist her through this process. In our culture, pregnancy was that slow process during which a woman gradually came to accept the fact that she was now sharing her bodily space with another, and that now, as well as for many years after the child was born, she was likely to have primary responsibility for this new person's well-being. If someone else wanted to find out how the embryo or fetus was doing, they had to ask her how she felt, look at her changing body, listen to it, and feel it— but all from the outside.

The fiber-optic photos of a fetus in the womb which Lennart Nilsson published in *Life* magazine in April 1965 were a tour de force, but they did not appreciably change this situation. The real change came about in the 1980s, with the increasingly routine use of "real time ultrasound," a method by which a fetus can be "observed" as it moves inside a pregnant woman's womb. This development has given "the fetus" a reality quite apart from that of the woman in whose flesh it is embedded. Indeed the miracle of ultrasound imaging is such that the fetus appears as though it were suspended in space. The woman is obliterated. She does not exist at all.

But, as the historian Barbara Duden has pointed out, there is an important difference between Nilsson's photographic images and the "images" provided by ultrasound.[1] Nilsson's pictures, startling as they were, bore a direct and immediately visible relationship to the captions with which he described them. Anyone looking at the pictures could see what the text said was there. Ultrasound images, by contrast, need to be interpreted by an experienced professional in order for an ordinary person, including the woman whose insides are being imaged, to "see" what is supposedly being shown. As Duden says, "Nothing seen...gives a clue as to what is photographed here." We must be told "that these clouds and masses...represent a human being."[2]

Thus, ultrasound imaging does not really render pregnant women transparent, because we do not literally *see* the fetus. We must be taught that we are seeing it. We are like travelers in a foreign land whose inhabitants speak a language we do not understand. We must accept what professional interpreters tell us about what they, the natives in the land of ultrasound imaging, see inside our bodies.

This means that physicians now have the power to guide our fantasies about what goes on in our womb. They can inform us whether the fetus's size and its anatomy seem appropriate for the time it has been developing and they can answer the all-important question of whether it is male or female, so that we, too, may now dutifully "see," or not see, a penis. (Note that Freud was right after all. What lets us know the fetus is female is that she does *not* have a penis.)

Once we know so much and our fantasies have been simultaneously expanded and circumscribed in this way, we may want to "know" more. This is where predictive diagnoses come in and where the alphabet soup of the As, Gs, Ts, and Cs that constitute DNA gets to increase our transparency, unveiling further secrets.

Nowadays a fetus not only gets to have its over-all anatomy surveyed, which saves us the trouble of fantasizing about our future baby's sex. We can also stop having fantasies (or nightmares) about her or his future health. Provided that we, or our insurers, are prepared to pay, we can have tests for a whole range of diseases and disabilities that may lie in the poor unborn creature's future.

Will he (remember, the fetus is no longer an "it") have one of the rather rare conditions whose trans-mission within families follows Mendel's laws of inheritance, such as cystic fibrosis? Or will she per-haps be at greater than average risk of developing one of the much more common conditions that sometimes appear to have familial components, say, diabetes or high blood pressure, later in life? And though we may know that the tests are still experi-mental and their predictive value is uncertain, and though we also may know in our hearts that no one can foretell what a person's life will be like, the test results have the power to reassure or frighten us.

Molecular biologists and the media keep saying that we are just read-outs of our genes and that the more we can find out about them, the more we will know about ourselves and our future children. In a burst of mindless enthusiasm, my Harvard colleague Walter Gilbert even assures us that all the genetic information about us will fit "on a single compact disk (CD), and one will be able to pull a CD out of one's pocket and say, 'Here is a human being; it's me!'"[3]

But, like ultrasound imaging, genetic predictions are only a way of interpreting data. The prognostications depend on establishing similarities and differences between measurements made on tissue samples obtained from the person or fetus being "diagnosed," compared with some reference standard. Much of medical diagnosis is like that: it structures reality around numbers, such as blood pressure or cholesterol levels. The interpretation of what the specific values mean changes from time to time, but the numbers continue to be considered significant and important. As the famous Soviet neurologist and psychologist Alexander Romanovich Luria commented:

> The physicians of our time, having a battery of auxiliary laboratory aids and tests, frequently overlook clinical reality. Observation of patients and evaluation of syndromes have begun to give way to dozens of laboratory analyses which are then combined by mathematical techniques as a means of diagnosis and as a plan of treatment."[4]

This criticism is highly relevant to DNA-based predictions, especially since they cover even more ground than most other diagnostic tests do. The future child's health will no longer be deduced from her appearance or reaction to stimuli after she has been born, but on what DNA tests have predicted about her. Her fate will be read in a new kind of tea leaves, which consist of the dark lines or blotches on film that are regularly shown in television programs about the wonders of the new genetics. (In those TV shows, no one ever says what the images mean. The point of letting us see them is just to imply that they are of enormous significance.)

As we saw earlier, in this culture, feelings of ill health—illness—are transformed into diseases when our subjective sensations become "symptoms" that can be fitted into diagnostic categories. And, like A.T. Luria, other critics of modern scientific medicine have complained that an ill person's chart has assumed greater significance than the way she or he feels.

With genetic predictions, prenatal or otherwise, the reliance on supposedly objective data goes even further. Once we have been shown to harbor some particular genetic variant, we need no longer feel bad or have symptoms in order to be diagnosed as diseased. We and our future children can then join the ever-growing number of "healthy ill." Eventually, that will include all of us who feel fine at present, but are predicted to develop a specific condition at an unspecified time in the future. Unless we prevent it, such a predictive test, interpreted to mean, for example, that a woman carries a genetic variant predisposing her to develop breast cancer, will be taken to mean she has cancer long before she has cancer.

In the context of procreation and pregnancy, this blurring means that a future child is labeled: she now *has* whatever condition tests predict she will (or rather, may) develop. That is how the obstetrician thinks of her, how the genetic counselor thinks of her, and how we ourselves are supposed to think of her. The only question is: what are we going to do about it?

This new way of looking at health and illness offers physicians a way to get around the well-known fact that all predictions, including medical predictions, are contingent and therefore uncertain. Few genetic predictions are absolute, and even if the child is born with the predicted condition, or develops it later, usually no one can predict how hampered or disabled not "the average child," but this particular child, living her or his specific life, will be. In other words, the apparent transparency of pregnant women is an illusion built, in part, on the fact that our culture exaggerates the knowledge value of medical tests and of the predictions they offer.

The problem can be illustrated with reference to sickle cell anemia, an inherited condition about whose mechanisms of genetic transmission and molecular pathology a great deal is known. As I mentioned earlier, people who inherit the relevant variant, usually called the "sickle cell gene," from only one of their parents experience no symptoms. Without the availability of a test, they would never know they have this allele. However, once that fact has been established, they are said to have sickle cell trait, a label that has no medical significance for them, though it may become relevant when they decide to have children. But it has led to genetic discrimination.[5] People who inherit two copies of this variant, one from each of their parents, are said to have sickle cell anemia.

However, contrary to common misperceptions, this label does not predict the appearance, extent, or frequency of symptoms. The reason is that the usual allele of which the "sickle cell gene" is a variant specifies the composition of the red blood protein hemoglobin. The "sickle cell gene" specifies the composition of a slightly different form of this protein, called hemoglobin-S (S is for sickle cell). Hemoglobin molecules are densely packed into our red blood cells and pick up oxygen in our lungs and release it as our blood circulates through the body. However, when hemoglobin-S molecules release their oxygen, they begin to stick to each other, which changes the usually round red blood cells to a sickle- or comma-like shape. Rather than pass smoothly through the network of our small capillary blood vessels, such sickled cells stack up and clog them. This, in turn, leads to the bleeding, pain, infections, and inflamed joints often associated with sickle cell anemia.

However, the point is that the extent to which these problems occur depends not only on the presence of hemoglobin-S in the blood. Many other factors influence what is going to happen: the total amount of hemoglobin in the red blood cells, the presence of other forms of hemoglobin, whether the person is dehydrated (which would increase the concentration of their red blood cells), the diameter of the blood vessels, the texture of their capillary walls, whether they are tense so that their blood vessels are unusually constricted, and so on. This is why different people experience sickle cell disease differently and why the same person experiences it differently at different times.

As I said earlier, nothing that happens in our bodies depends on the way one single kind of gene functions. Different kinds of genes are involved in everything, as are different kinds of proteins, and a lot of other circumstances within our bodies and in our environment. It is more useful to think of our bodies and our health as ecological systems with many different components, interacting in a multiplicity of ways, than to conceptualize ourselves as read-outs of a genetic program.

Only rarely does a genetic prediction or diagnosis make it possible to specify the time course and severity of the associated condition. The situation that is usually cited as an example is Tay Sachs disease, which at present, indeed, invariably leads to the neurological deterioration and early death of children who inherit the specific variant gene from both their parents. But Tay Sachs disease represents an exception that should not be generalized.

Particularly when we consider the more common conditions, such as cancer, Alzheimer disease, hypertension, diabetes, and the various behavioral disorders, we are never speaking about a single, unique mutation in a specific gene, even when there seems to be a familial component. It is always a question of multiple internal and external events coming together to elicit the disease processes and their symptoms. Equating the identification of a genetic variant with the existence of a disease, irrespective of the presence or absence of symptoms, encourages us to ignore the obvious variability in the incidence and character of the relevant conditions.

So, just as women have not really become transparent, genes have not really become visible and predictive. What has happened is that medical geneticists have begun to redefine the concept of disease to represent what DNA-based tests predict about us. But this definition ignores the host of circumstances that affect our health in addition to what our genes may contribute.

The incidence of cancer in New Jersey or Maryland is much higher than that in Utah or Wyoming not because of differences in the genes that people who live in these states inherit from their parents. Nor is the crime rate in U.S. metropolitan areas more than three times what it is in rural counties because of differences in the genes of city and country people. And the fact that death rates for newborns and infants in the United States exceed those in every other industrially developed country and in some so-called Third World countries, such as Barbados and Cuba, also is not due to genes.

Geneticization threatens not only our individual sense of health and well-being; it whittles away at our social cohesiveness. Once prenatal predictions are available, what children will a cost-conscious society allow to be born? And who will make those decisions? To reduce U.S. infant mortality rates does not require that we look into women's bodies and visualize genes. But it does require profound changes in our current social and economic arrangements because it requires that everyone have enough food of the proper kind, a decent place to live, satisfying work to do, and hope for the future, along with an education that includes appropriate sex education, and health care that includes access to contraception, abortion, and prenatal and well-baby care.

Such an outlook implies the very opposite of

the current overemphasis on the implications of genetics for individual health, because it requires a sense of responsibility for each other and a determination to raise everyone's level of well-being. This may sound impossibly idealistic, but is, in fact, a lot like what the Labour government put in place when the British entered on their modern welfare state in the mid-1940s.

The present move in the direction of geneticization draws attention and resources away from the basic necessities for healthful living. While we gaze in fascination into some women's bellies, hoping to foresee the health of their future children, we close our eyes to the lack of the basic preconditions for health and the public health needs of infants, children, and adults living in our midst.

It is an enormous waste of talent and resources to try to foresee the potential health hazards that lurk in the genes of each of us while entire segments of the U.S. and world population are exposed to wholly visible threats to their health and well-being. By shifting attention away from these needs, the current genomania actually threatens health.

Of course, it is far easier to blame people's genes than to abolish the sources of victimization. And it also generates profits for the scientists and biotechnology companies that are developing and marketing the tests. But if we really want to improve public welfare and health, we must come out of the genetic house of mirrors, look at the realities that stare us in the face, and do something about them.

Genes and Behavior

Defining Behaviors

"Dissolved in a test tube, the essence of life is a clear liquid."

So opens the cover story about the wonders of DNA in the January 17, 1994 issue of *Time* magazine.[1] In the face of such a poetic claim, how can I dare question the decisive influence of genes on behavior? And yet, I propose to show that attempts to identify genes as "essences" that determine behavior are problematic from beginning to end.

In the first place, behaviors are not attributes of individuals. Behavior is something that happens between people and in a context. This is why Harvard psychiatrist Erich Lindemann used to say: "It is a fiction that mental illness resides within the individual."[2] Behavior also gets interpreted in a context. The criteria used to define behaviors, to lump them into categories, and to decide which of them are to be called beneficial or normal and which detrimental or pathological depend on a great many cultural assumptions. Take competitiveness as an example. In capitalist societies, it is considered "normal," and indeed laudable, for men to be highly competitive. Competitive women, however, until recently—and in many places still now—are subject to psychiatric control.

The classification and naming of behaviors, as though they were discrete traits with a clear-cut identity, rests on what Alfred North Whitehead called the fallacy of misplaced concreteness. Drinking too much alcohol, preferring to have sexual or love relationships with members of one's own sex, or seeing or hearing what others cannot see or hear are not discrete "characters" or "traits," like the flower colors of Mendel's pea plants or the shapes of their seeds. What we call alcoholism, homosexuality, or schizophrenia obviously incorporates cultural assumptions and conventions.

This is why the Indian psychiatrist Ajita Chakraborty believes that psychiatry needs to build in an anthropological perspective. He points out that, though British and U.S. psychiatrists live and are trained within similar traditions, they "differ widely in their diagnosis of schizophrenia" and not just by virtue of differences in "local semantics," but on "conceptual and cultural" grounds. Turning to India, he suggests that differences in the kinds of work, working conditions, and attitudes to work may be why "Indian society is more tolerant [of schizophrenia than Western, industrialized countries are], and perhaps allows a patient to recover without specific interventions.... Illnesses, tensions, and conflicts are frequently contained and resolved...through existing in-built cultural processes."[3]

Even staying within a single, ethnically fairly homogeneous country, researchers analyzing data from Sweden have found that the incidence of schizophrenia is 1.65 times higher among male conscripts who have grown up in cities than among those who grew up in the countryside. The researchers do not pretend to know why this is so but, after controlling for differences in such potentially stressful experiences as drug use and parental divorce, they conclude that the difference may be due to the greater overall number of "stressful life-events" to which boys who grow up in cities are exposed, as compared with those living in rural areas.[4]

Whatever the specific reasons for these kinds of national and regional differences may be, social environment and cultural values clearly affect the incidence, as well as the interpretation and diagnosis, of the behaviors that get classified as schizophrenia or other forms of mental illness.

Molecular Interpretations of Behavior

Because behaviors are assigned different values, molecular scientists do not find all behaviors equally interesting. Though everything people do involves our physiology, and therefore our genes, scientists tend only to look for the genetic components of behaviors to which their society assigns importance and which it thinks are probably hereditary, such as homosexuality, alcoholism, or schizophrenia and other forms of "mental illness." But since such behaviors are not any one thing, how can specific variations in DNA sequences "cause" the conglomerations of behaviors to which we attach discrete names? Furthermore, as David and Henri Cohen point out, since "we lack the most rudimentary conceptions of how so-called normal behavior is linked to neurochemical processes," how can we expect to understand which ones of these processes are changed, or how or whether they are changed, in so-called abnormal or otherwise stigmatized behaviors?[5]

Molecular biologists try to circumvent such problems by assuming that specific biochemical pathways, involving specific enzymes, receptors, or other proteins, whose composition is, of course, specified by genes, underlie the different and more global manifestations of these behaviors. Alcoholism thus gets reduced to malfunctioning dopamine receptors,[6] homosexuality to brain structures or hormones,[7] schizophrenia to dopamine receptors or receptors for other neurotransmitters, or if not receptors, then some other proteins involved with brain metabolism.[8] More recently, molecular biologists are taking the short-cut of not implicating specific metabolic pathways at all, but simply looking for correlations between specific variants in DNA sequences and the behavior in question.[9] Yet, for such correlations to be meaningful and predictive, it becomes all the more crucial to delineate the "abnormal" or stigmatized behavior precisely and to distinguish it clearly from its "normal" or socially accepted counterpart.

Definitions of Mental Illness

I want now to narrow this discussion to "mental illness." As Michel Foucault pointed out, the concept of madness arose, historically, as the antithesis of reason.[10] And the more precious and precarious the pursuit of reason, the more threatening become the possibilities of madness. But clearly, different cultures differ in where they set the boundaries between reason and madness, or sanity and insanity, and in the shape they give those boundaries. For example, though in the United States we no longer permit "sane" people to see visions or hear voices, the sight of "extraterrestrial" machines, such as UFOs or flying saucers, does not necessarily label one as crazy. We might also ask with Lily Tomlin, "Why is it that when we talk to God, we are said to be praying, and when God talks to us, we're said to be schizophrenic?"

Our insistence on understanding the origin, or cause, of madness—which at present means the molecular variations, or genes, associated with it—is probably driven by anxiety that we ourselves may be mad and merely not know it. It is reassuring, then, to find out which gene is broken in people who are mad because, if ours is whole, we ourselves need not fear being or becoming mad.

In preparation for writing this essay, I have been reading some of the current crop of autobiographical reflections by people who have been labeled autistic,[11,12] schizophrenic,[13] or manic depressive.[14] What emerges is that these people differ from me as a matter of degree and at some times, but that the differences between us are not like those between Mendel's pea flowers. These authors do not have red petals, while mine are white. I can recognize myself in a great deal of what these writers describe, as can other readers, which is why several of the books have become best sellers.

D.L. Rosenhan's classic *Science* paper shows that psychiatrists have no definitive criteria for distinguishing who is sane or insane. In this experiment, Rosenhan and seven confederates—three women and five men—tried to get admitted as patients at twelve hospitals in five states on the East and West coasts of the United States. After telephoning for an appointment, at the admission interview the only "symptom" they complained of was that they had been hearing voices, which they described as "often unclear," but as far as they could tell, the voices said "empty," "hollow," and "thud." In other ways and from that point on, each behaved as she or he would normally.

To their surprise, none of the "pseudo-patients" (as Rosenhan calls them) had trouble getting admitted, but all had some difficulty getting released. They ended up spending between 7 and 52 days in hospital (an average of 19 days). The "pseudo-patients" were constantly taking notes, which was among the things that led the other inmates to decide that they were only pretending to be crazy. But none of the professionals with whom they had contact questioned that they were indeed insane, and when they were finally released, their release forms described them not as sane or cured, but as "in remission." One must wonder why it was so easy for the other inmates to see through the hoax, while none of the professionals did.[15]

Genes Known to Affect Behavior

Please do not take what I am saying to mean that I think genes do not affect behavior. We have known for decades about certain gene mutations that influence intelligence and behavior and that are transmitted in families in the predictable patterns described by Mendel's laws. I am thinking of the mutations involved in PKU (phenylketonuria), which is characterized by mental retardation, or Huntington disease, which results in disorientation, mental deterioration, and insanity. However, the point is that no one could have predicted that either of these mutations would result in mental symptoms.

The inactivation of the enzyme, whose composition is determined by the allele associated with PKU, results in the accumulation of the amino acid phenylalanine and of its metabolic products. This has many effects, and the imbalances in brain function that result in the mental retardation associated with PKU are among them, but this effect could not have been predicted.

The variation in DNA associated with Huntington disease is usually not expressed until mid-life. This, too, could not have been predicted. As yet, no one knows the identity or function of the protein (recently named huntingtin) which is associated with the "normal" gene much less the way in which its malfunctioning, or failure to function, leads to the snow-balling symptoms of Huntington disease.

Genes and their variants do not function as parts of simple, linear pathways. In fact, this is true also of malfunctions of much less complicated molecules than DNA or proteins. Think of niacin, or nicotinamide, a member of the vitamin B complex. There was no way to *predict* that a deficiency of this vitamin, which is essential to the metabolism of cells all over the body, would give rise to the specific symptoms of pellagra, including its mental and behavioral ones.

Gene Expression and Disease

The point is that cellular metabolism is full of alternative pathways and redundancies. Which molecules or reactions are critical, and the circumstances under which they will be so, cannot be predicted from first principles. As I have said before, even with conditions whose patterns of inheritance can be predicted by Mendel's laws, such as sickle cell anemia (SCA) or cystic fibrosis (CF), the situation is far from simple.

For example, though the gene associated with CF has been identified much more recently than the "SCA gene," already some 350 different variations in its base sequence have been found to be associated with symptoms of cystic fibrosis. Depending on the identity of the specific variation, the symptoms range from mild to severe. Furthermore, some of these same variations have been identified also among people who do not have the condition.[16] This means that the existence of variations in the "CF gene" that are associated with CF in some people cannot be used to predict this condition in everyone.

Even more surprising are recent experiments in which mouse embryos, in whom a gene considered essential for growth and development was knocked out completely, were born quite normal.[17,18] Indeed, some such animals have reproduced normal offspring for several generations.[19] This means that, even for clearly defined ailments, identifying the associated gene variant(s) does not predict the severity of the condition or even that it will occur at all.

DNA-Based Diagnoses

Even if it were possible to link specific variants of DNA to, let us say, schizophrenia and to establish that some forms of schizophrenia have a familial component, the presence of such variants could never be used to predict who will or will not develop symptoms. But having a physician predict that I am liable to develop schizophrenia could affect the course of my life and thus my chances of developing symptoms of schizophrenia and, perhaps especially, my chances of being diagnosed as exhibiting such symptoms.

To establish the predictive validity of supposed genetic markers for a particular health condition, it is not enough to show that these markers are present among people diagnosed to have the condition. One also needs to show that they are absent in people who do not have it. Because they ignored this fact, Patricia Jacobs and her colleagues years ago made the mistake of drawing a causal connection between the XYY chromosomal condition and criminal behavior.[20]

As we have seen, unfortunately, now that DNA tests are available, molecular biologists and diagnosticians could simply decide to count the DNA marker itself as the diagnostic symptom—in other words, to redefine what it means to "have" the condition. Especially for conditions that are hard to define, that would be very convenient. I no longer need to exhibit symptoms. If I have the DNA marker, I will be diagnosed as sick with the associated condition: invisible genes become one with visible traits.

Indeed, if the principal intent is not to improve diagnosis and treatment, but to prevent people from being born who might be at greater than usual risk to develop certain conditions, then to detect the presence of supposedly predictive DNA markers would be quite enough. In our democratic times, this eugenic goal could be achieved even without eugenic health courts, like those of the Nazi period. The authorities would simply need to inform prospective parents that their future child has a genetic marker with dire implications and let them "choose" what to do. (By way of public concern and fiscal prudence, governments might, of course, enact legislation that stipulates that, once future parents are forewarned, they cannot expect to "burden" society with the expense of caring for whatever disability their child has been predicted to develop.)

The fact that, twenty or thirty years down the road, these "preventive measures" are not likely to have had much of an impact on the incidence of conditions such as schizophrenia will not differentiate these novel diagnostic and "therapeutic" interventions from the more conventional ones.

"Mental Illness"
Does Not Reside in Individuals

There is no question that DNA (genes) must affect behavior and mental functioning. We know that the sequence of bases in DNA influences the composition and structure of all proteins, including the specific ones required for our mental, as well as physical, well-being. (Indeed, I look upon "mental" and "physical" as complementary and inseparable.) But what is it that genes "for" behaviors of various types are genes for? Various receptor molecules that interact with neurotransmitters? Enzymes involved in the synthesis or metabolism of one or another neurotransmitter? Proteins involved in the synthesis, release, or uptake of hormones or other molecules that help to organize our brain and senses throughout our lives? Since all of these, and more, are involved in our mental functioning, it will not be difficult to find genes linked to behaviors. The difficulty will lie in the overwhelming *embarras de richesse*.

So, obviously, genes participate in all our mental and physical functions. But the point is that information about variations in DNA sequences is not useful for predicting, or diagnosing, mental or physical dysfunctions, and does not have therapeutic value. Furthermore, predicting mental (dys)functions is more dangerous than predicting, say, the occurrence of sickle cell anemia, because our moods, emotions, and mental functions are influenced by our own expectations as well as by those of our family, friends, teachers, and caregivers—in fact, by the expectations of everyone who is aware of the predictions.

To come back to where I began. Our psyches are not ours alone; they connect us with the world. Therefore, our own and other people's expectations of our future affect that future as well as the present.

Ever subtler levels of prediction and classification, such as genes and DNA, cannot substitute for the social and psychological help people need in times of stress and pain. But more than that, the renewed focus on genes weakens the fabric that holds families and societies together by individualizing responsibilities for the breakdown of what are at their core interpersonal and social relationships.

Canceling a Conference on "Genetics and Crime"

Censorship or Scientific Responsibility?

Written with Elijah Wald

On July 15, 1992, the National Institutes of Health (NIH) froze funds amounting to $78,000 which had been allocated to support a conference to be held October 9-11 of that year at the University of Maryland's Institute for Philosophy and Public Policy. In September, the conference was defunded altogether. Since NIH director Dr. Bernadine P. Healy was involved in both decisions, it is important to explore whether her actions constitute government censorship and infringement of academic freedom or whether she used her authority appropriately.

Opposition to the conference began to build among biomedical and social scientists and public interest groups soon after the conference brochure was mailed out early in June. The conference was called "Genetic Factors in Crime: Findings, Uses & Implications" and the brochure opened with the sentence "Researchers have already begun to study the genetic regulation of violent and impulsive behavior and to search for genetic markers associated with criminal conduct." The first paragraph ended: "Genetic research holds out the prospect of identifying individuals who may be predisposed to certain kinds of criminal conduct, of isolating environmental features which trigger those predispositions, and of treating some predispositions with drugs and unintrusive therapies."

These words were enough to set off warning bells among people aware of the long history of so-called scientific attempts to link crime to an individual's biological make-up. Efforts to predict criminal tendencies in the past have focused on a person's facial features or body build, or on the XYY chromosomal constitution of a small percentage of men. So far, all such links have been shown to be false and often absurd. Currently genes are in vogue as potential predictors of behavior. There have been claims of genes not just "for" alcoholism and mental illness, but also "for" shyness and the tendency to begin smoking and not be able to stop. So why not for crime?

Most of this research is based on comparisons of identical twins and ordinary siblings. Such studies are notoriously unreliable since identical twins have a great deal more in common than their genes. It is never possible to disentangle the biological and social components of complex behaviors and twin studies cannot solve this methodological problem. As Harvard population geneticist Richard Lewontin points out, "There is a strong effort on the part of parents of many twins to make them as similar as possible. They are given names beginning with the same letter and are dressed alike. International twin conventions give prizes for the most similar twins."[1] Are there genes for wearing matched pink and white party dresses?

It is important to understand that, despite the fact that people commit lots of different crimes, only certain crimes get linked to genes. No one tries to identify genes for committing S & L fraud, insurance scams, or perjury when testifying before Congress. Genes are invoked for crimes of violence that conjure up racist stereotypes. Yet, it makes little sense to look for genes that trigger criminal behavior in someone growing up in an urban slum where drug dealers are the only people with money.

Any attempt to biologize criminal behavior locates the problem inside the person and draws attention away from obvious economic and social reasons why certain groups of people, identifiable by race and class, are disproportionately likely to populate our prisons. Not every law-breaker gets caught, arrested, indicted, or convicted, but among the factors leading to arrests or convictions, race is high on the list. The FBI reports that in 1991 black youths were arrested at five times the rate of white youths, and at present more young black men are in prisons and jails than in college. Neither statistic is merely a function of who breaks the law.

In the discussions surrounding the defunding of the conference on "Genetic Factors in Crime" surprisingly little attention has focused on who gets labeled "criminal" and what activities get called crimes. Nor has sufficient attention been drawn to the fact that access to resources, such as the ability to mount an elaborate defense, makes it far less likely that an affluent law-breaker will end up a convicted felon than will someone who must cut costs by copping a plea. Given the complexities of who gets labeled a criminal and the difficulties of reliably linking genes and behavior, what conceivable scientific merit can there be in looking for "genetic factors in crime" or in holding out the promises made in the conference brochure about the potential for identification, diagnosis, and "unintrusive therapies" for individuals "predisposed to certain kinds of criminal conduct"?

Conference organizer David Wasserman has written that he was merely trying to set the stage for open discussion, but discussions of biological factors in crime are necessarily mired in ideological preconceptions and racist prejudices. It is unfortunate that the review panel which approved the application to fund the conference did not recognize that the very definition of what constitutes "criminal behavior" is flawed and that it is impossible to disentangle potential "genetic components" of crime from a wide range of societal effects. It seems entirely appropriate that Dr. Healy, as head of a government funding agency, should have been responsive to public criticism and decided that a conference built on this kind of quicksand would not benefit science, the public interest, or the NIH, and that it therefore should not be supported at public expense.

Gay Genes?

Written with Elijah Wald

Gay genes are back in the news. Researchers from the National Cancer Institute announced in the July 16, 1993 issue of the journal *Science* that they have found a set of genetic markers shared by a number of gay brothers, indicating genetic roots of homosexuality. This study, like similar previous findings, is flawed. It is based on simplistic assumptions about sexuality and is hampered by the near impossibility of establishing links between genes and behavior.

The authors of the article claim to have found that 33 of the 40 pairs of gay brothers in their study shared certain DNA sequences on their X chromosome, the chromosome men inherit only from their mothers. The implicit reasoning is that if brothers who have specific DNA sequences in common are both gay, these sequences can be considered genetic markers for homosexuality.

There are problems with this reasoning. Of the relatively small number of siblings in the survey, almost a quarter did not have these markers. Also, the researchers did not do the obvious control experiment of checking for the presence of these markers among heterosexual brothers of the gay men they studied. It is surprising that the correlation found in this research warranted publication without these controls, especially in as influential a journal as *Science*.

Past claims of the discovery of genetic markers

for behavioral traits such as schizophrenia, manic depression, and alcoholism have not withstood further investigation. The reason the gay gene "discovery" is big news is not that it is any more promising than the others but that the debate on homosexual rights is hot. The *Science* article came fast on the heels of the gays-in-the-military debate and controversial referenda on gay rights in Colorado and Oregon.

The new findings, which have been heralded as a striking breakthrough in our understanding of sexuality, conform to a long-established pattern. Although people have been sexually attracted to their own sex throughout history, our current perception of homosexuality is rooted in the late 19th century. At that time, sexual activities were first used to define the people who engaged in them. Any sexual act that deviated from the "missionary position" could lead to its practitioner being stamped a "pervert." Masturbators, it was said, could be recognized on sight by their sallow and nervous appearance. Homosexuality stopped being what people did and became who they were. As the French philosopher Michel Foucault wrote, "The sodomite had been a temporary aberration; the homosexual was now a species."

This way of categorizing people obscured the accepted fact that many people do not have sexual relations exclusively in one way or with either sex. Turn-of-the-century sex reformers such as Havelock Ellis, while understanding that the categories could blur, began viewing homosexuals as biologically different from heterosexuals. They argued that homosexuals should not be punished for their acts because their orientation was biological, not a matter of choice.

Similarly, in the face of virulent homophobic attacks, some homosexuals and their allies now argue that if sexual orientation is not a choice but is biologically determined, discrimination against homosexuals would best be covered by civil rights laws.

But the use of the phrase "sexual orientation" to describe only a person's having sex with members of their own, or the other, sex obscures the fact that many of us have other strong and consistent sexual orientations—toward certain hair colors, body shapes, racial types. It would be as logical to look for genes associated with these orientations as for "homosexual genes."

Still, many people believe that homosexuality would be more socially accepted if it were shown to be inborn. The late gay journalist Randy Shiltz said that a biological explanation "would reduce being gay to something like being left-handed, which is in fact all that it is."

This argument is not very convincing. Until the latter half of this century, left-handed people were often forced to switch over and were punished if they continued to favor their "bad" hand. Grounding difference in biology does not stem bigotry. African Americans, Jews, people with disabilities, as well as homosexuals have been persecuted for their biological "flaws." The Nazis exterminated such people precisely to prevent them from "contaminating" the Aryan gene pool. Despite claims to the contrary, this attitude hasn't disappeared: *The Daily Mail* of London reported on the *Science* article under the headline "Abortion Hope After 'Gay Genes' Findings."

PROFITABLE PROMISES

Social movements can generate interest in, and support for, science. Just as the civil rights movement led to research on racial differences and the women's movement to research on male-female differences, the search for gay genes comes directly out of the successes of the gay rights struggle. But studies of human biology cannot explain the wide range of human behaviors. Such efforts fail to acknowledge that sexual attraction depends on personal experience and cultural values and that sexual desire is too complex, varied, and interesting to be reduced to genes.

Part II

Women, Science and Power

Introduction to Part II

The essays in this section were written over more years and cover more diverse subjects than those in Part I. Yet, they all illustrate the ways often prestigious scientists, physicians, and, in the final essay, legal experts use their expert knowledge to reinforce, or at least support, conservative opinions about women's place in society.

The first essay was initially delivered as an invited talk at a meeting of the American Association for the Advancement of Science, and discusses current approaches to three important areas in women's health—breast cancer, AIDS, and occupational health.

The essay entitled "Sexism and Sociobiology" was written for an edited collection, intended as part of a "countercelebration" on the occasion of the 350th anniversary of the founding of Harvard University. Hence its preoccupation with two Harvard "greats," the physician Edward H. Clarke and the biologist Edward O. Wilson. About one hundred years apart, these two professors wrote popular books that lent scientific respectability to sexist practices and opinions of their time. This is the reason for the ad hominem nature of this essay which should not be taken to imply that these two men, or their theories, have had a unique place in the history of scientific sexism. Fuller accounts of this fascinating subject have appeared in Steven J. Gould's *Mismeasure of Man*, Anne Fausto-Sterling's *Myths of Gender*, and my *Politics of Women's Biology*, among other books and articles. I have included the essay here because it is important to keep reminding ourselves that prestigious scientists and other scholars of note have a history of producing, or reinforcing, ideologies that legitimate oppressive practices.

The review of a book about abortion is included to make the similar point that natural scientists and other scholars can be surprisingly unaware of the limited applicability of their expert knowledge to real life situations. While granting that an embryo or fetus is "alive" from the moment of conception, the authors of this book invent a quaint concept of "humanness," supposedly based in biology, for the purpose of having a scientific marker for when a fetus becomes "human." The problem is that, throughout, they keep their gaze fixed on "the fetus," while ignoring the fact that pregnancy involves *two* human lives.

A rather novel, but equally explicit, cultural use of "the fetus" to control women is discussed in the final essay, which focuses on the recent implication that a conflict of interests exists between pregnant women and the fetuses they harbor in their bodies. Like the current efforts to control women's decisions about childbearing by manipulating welfare payments, "fetal/maternal conflicts" are cruel inventions, used almost exclusively against poor women.

Women's Health

Some New Wrinkles on Some Old Issues

Biologists and physicians have traditionally been men and have thought of males as the norm. And they have taught us to think of the ways in which women's bodies are different from men's as deviations from this norm. As a result, such normal functions as menstruation, pregnancy, childbirth, and menopause have been needlessly medicalized. At present in the United States, approximately one in four births involves major abdominal surgery—a Caesarean—and some physicians consider normal menopause a hormone deficiency disease for which they routinely prescribe estrogen supplements.

Pregnancy and birth occupy a smaller and smaller portion of women's lives. Yet, the term "women's health" conjures up images of procreation rather than of the conditions that most plague women. Little research has been done on lupus, rheumatoid arthritis, scleroderma, and other conditions that affect primarily women. No one even understands why their incidence is skewed. Meanwhile, conditions that affect women and men in roughly equal numbers, such as high blood pressure, heart disease, and many types of cancer, have been studied almost exclusively in men. The course these conditions take in women has not been documented and physicians do not really know what dosages of accepted remedies to prescribe for women or even whether these remedies are appropriate.

These problems have led some women's health activists to suggest that "women's health" become a new medical specialty that includes all health issues relevant to women, including concerns related to procreation. I do not want to enter this debate here. Instead I shall discuss three current health concerns for women: breast cancer, AIDS, and occupational health.

Breast Cancer

In the United States, cancer is the second highest cause of death (the first being diseases of the heart and circulatory system). The top cause of cancer mortality for men is lung cancer. Among women, lung and breast cancer vie for first place.

In 1991, the American Cancer Society publicized the statistic that an American woman's risk of getting breast cancer is 1 in 9, and changed that to 1 in 8 in 1992. Popular articles on breast cancer tend to emphasize that women should start watching for signs of breast cancer as early as their forties, or even in their thirties, and many young women think the 1 in 8 figure is relevant to their present lives. However, breast cancer includes a variety of cancerous conditions, most of which only affect older women.

The 1 in 8 figure does not mean that if eight women are tested, one will turn out to have breast cancer. It represents the cumulative probability that a given woman will develop breast cancer some time in her life. In fact, the probability that a 35-year-old woman will develop breast cancer by the time she is

55 is about 1 in 40, and the probability that she will die from it by 55 is about 1 in 180.

Even for older women, the probability of developing breast cancer at any one time never gets nearly as high as 1 in 8. For a woman of 40, the likelihood that she will test positive for breast cancer before the year's end is about 1 in 1000, and even for a woman of 60 that likelihood is only about 1 in 500. So, the numbers the American Cancer Society is putting out are misleading, and intentionally so. One of their spokespersons was quoted in the *New York Times* of March 15, 1992 as saying that the statistics are "meant to be a jolt" and "to remind people that the problem hasn't gone away." But it is bad policy to use scare tactics, because they are likely to make people distrustful or fatalistic.

The numbers the American Cancer Society and cancer specialists put out about breast cancer are also problematic because they are based on statistical averages. Yet, each of us is concerned about herself and other specific women, not about a fictitious "average woman." The probability that any particular woman will get breast cancer is said to depend on her so-called "risk factors." But before we get too enthusiastic about risk-factor-based predictions, we need to understand that most women who get breast cancer have no known risk factors at all, and having one or another "risk factor" does not mean that a woman will develop cancer, only that her chances of doing so may be higher than average.

The current list of risk factors is compiled from studies conducted by different researchers, using different criteria and methods. Before placing too much weight on them, we must learn a good deal

91

more than we now know about the way women's breasts change throughout life and about the relationships between these processes and the way women live: the structural and functional correlates of beginning, and ceasing, to menstruate and the age at which this occurs; of sexual habits; of whether and at what age women first get pregnant and whether they carry that pregnancy to term; of whether and how long they breastfeed; and so on.

Women's breasts are not made of marble. They are complex organs that consist of different kinds of tissues and change in the course of a woman's life. The reason they are susceptible to developing cancer is that some of our tissues, such as the cells lining the milk ducts, continue dividing even after we have stopped growing. To understand why cancers start and spread, it would be important to know how environmental, social, nutritional, and other factors affect the development and metabolism of the various types of breast tissue.

For example, women's breasts are rich in fatty tissue, which concentrates fat-soluble substances. Some of these, such as PCBs, PBBs, and breakdown products of DDT, are known to be carcinogenic. But scientific or news accounts raise alarm only when these substances are shown to contaminate breast milk, owing to the hazard this poses for nursing infants. They rarely mention that such carcinogens are also hazardous for the lactating woman. Some studies point to a link between high concentrations of these chemicals in breast milk or breast tissue and breast cancer.

Radiation is another well-known environmental carcinogen. Yet, the American Cancer Society, the

National Cancer Institute, and other cancer specialists keep urging women to get mammograms at ever more frequent intervals and younger ages. Occasionally, a voice is raised warning that mammograms may be dangerous to some women who are particularly sensitive to radiation. The rationale for advising women to have frequent mammograms is the hope that early detection will prevent breast cancer from spreading into vital organs, such as the liver or lungs. But the data on that are equivocal. Most disturbing of all is the fact that, despite ever earlier detection and therapeutic interventions, the death rate from breast cancer (that is, the number of women dying in proportion to their total number in the population) has not changed in more than fifty years.

It would be far better to expand cancer prevention than early detection programs. And by prevention I do not mean the kind of large-scale experiment the National Cancer Institute has recently initiated. As part of this study, physicians are giving healthy young women thought to be at special risk for breast cancer a drug called tamoxifen. Until recently this medication has been given to women who have had breast cancer, because it appears to decrease the likelihood of a recurrence. However, tamoxifen itself is known to elicit blood-clotting problems and to increase the incidence of uterine and liver cancers and other liver diseases. It also can evoke hot flashes, vaginal bleeding, menstrual irregularities, and possibly cataracts. This is why the National Women's Health Network and a number of American cancer specialists have opposed this study as too risky.

The American Cancer Society and segments of the biomedical profession and associated industries may exaggerate the risk of breast cancer as part of the excessive medicalization of biological character-istics specific to women that I mentioned at the start. However, manufacturers of mammography machines and of tamoxifen and other "preventive" drugs and devices stand to make a healthy profit off women's fears of this cancer.

Rather than treat women with potentially car-cinogenic drugs or radiation as a way to prevent their getting breast cancer, it would be better to minimize exposure to known carcinogens, such as food additives and, above all, nuclear power plants. But most of all, we need to learn much more about the correlation of various biological and environ-mental factors with the incidence of breast cancer. Fortunately, some women's community cancer pro-jects have begun to agitate for this kind of epidemio-logical research, instead of concentrating on means for early detection such as mammography and, more recently, DNA-based testing.

The other two stories I want to look at illustrate different aspects of societal and medical neglect, rather than exaggeration, of women's illnesses. Let us start by looking at AIDS.

Women and AIDS

The incidence of infection with the Human Immunodeficiency Virus (HIV) and of the Acquired Immune Deficiency Syndrome (AIDS) is increasing dramatically among American women and especially among poor women, disproportionate numbers of whom are women of color. These women are being infected through sharing needles when injecting drugs and during heterosexual intercourse, when women are considerably more likely to be infected with HIV than to transmit the virus. Yet, medical and popular attention is focused primarily on two groups of women—prostitutes and pregnant women. The questions that are debated most assiduously are not how to protect women from becoming infected, and how to keep infected women healthy and alive for their own sakes, but how to keep them from becoming "vectors" of infection to men and babies.

In *Women and AIDS: The Invisible Epidemic*, Gena Corea recounts the medical neglect of women with HIV or AIDS. She points out that unusually large numbers of young, drug-addicted women began dying of various respiratory infections as early as 1981. This was the year the U.S. Centers for Disease Control (CDC) first warned that an unusual number of gay men were dying from Kaposi sarcoma and pneumocystis pneumonia, which led to AIDS being recognized as a syndrome. A dozen years later, these first women's deaths still are not counted as AIDS-related. And even though the death rates of young and middle-aged women in states and cities with a high prevalence of AIDS rose dramatically between 1981 and 1986, their deaths were usually attributed to respiratory and other infections, rather than to AIDS. The CDC did not list a disease of women in its definition of AIDS until the end of 1992, when it named invasive cervical cancer, although physicians caring for HIV-infected women had been reporting for years that among these women cervical cancer proliferates with such speed that annual Pap smears do not offer adequate warning.

The 1992 definition also included recurrent pneumonia and a low count of T4 white blood cells, which has expanded the number of women officially counted as having AIDS. This is important not just to maintain accurate health statistics, but to give these women access to needed medical and social services. But recurrent vaginal yeast infections and other gynecological symptoms in HIV-positive women still have not been included, even though health workers caring for at-risk women recognize these as likely indicators of HIV-disease.

Women have been neglected also in research protocols designed to explore the natural history of AIDS, so that many physicians still are unaware of the progression of AIDS-related infections in women and fail to recognize the warning signs. The assumption underlying this neglect is that the infection progresses the same way in women and men, which is not true. The other ostensible reason, which contradicts this assumption, is the same as the rationale that has been put forward for excluding women from other medical studies: that since women are different from men, their inclusion in the research population will confuse the data. Also, the reason often given for excluding women from drug studies is that the drug might endanger a "potential" fetus, should the woman be pregnant.

Gena Corea has described several well-designed studies on AIDS in women, proposed by experienced researchers between 1982 and 1990, for which funding was refused by the CDC and other government granting agencies. Studies have only now been initiated in which relatively large numbers of HIV-positive and negative women, with comparable demographic characteristics, are being tracked to define the course of the infection, the kinds of AIDS-related diseases women are likely to get, and how to treat them. In the present state of ignorance, no one even knows to what extent the T4 cell count put forward by the CDC in 1992 is relevant to women, since the normal range among different groups of women has not been established.

However, while a great deal of research is needed, protecting women against AIDS is going to take more than information, education, and medication. By and large, the women who are getting infected are among the most vulnerable women in society. They are not likely to be able to negotiate terms of sexual relationships or drug use with their partners. Recent research suggests that a disproportionate number of infected women have been sexually or physically abused from an early age. To address warnings about the need for condoms to these women, or indeed to any women, rather than to men, shows that society does not hold men accountable for their actions. As long as that is the case, while women continue to be less powerful than men—culturally as well as physically—women's infection rates are bound to increase.

A final word about maternal transmission of HIV. In the United States, the risk that the child of an HIV-infected woman would be born infected was initially estimated at over 60 percent. But as more has been learned, the probability of infection is now put at about 30 percent, and a large European study published in 1991 puts it at 13 percent. Here, as always, the person about whom health care workers should be concerned is the woman. No one is sure how or why the virus is transmitted in some pregnancies and not in others, but whatever the reasons, it makes sense to enable women to be properly nourished and housed and as healthy as possible during pregnancy as well as before and after it.

There have been recent reports that AZT and some vaccines reduce the transmission of the virus from pregnant women to their fetuses. Such clues need to be explored, but it is always important to consider the health of the women themselves as well as that of their future children.

Since injectable drugs are a main avenue of HIV transmission, women also need ready access to drug treatment programs. But unfortunately, few U.S. treatment programs accept women and even fewer accept pregnant women. Once again, attention focuses on "the fetus," and the question becomes, whether drug treatment might harm it, irrespective of whether the women would benefit. Similarly, the question gets raised of whether pregnant women who are infected with HIV or have AIDS should be permitted to take anti-AIDS drugs or to participate in drug trials. There is no evidence that the drugs in current use pose a greater threat to a fetus than the infection itself does and, as I said, AZT even seems to be beneficial, but to err on the side of caution, some physicians advise women not to take medication during the first trimester of a pregnancy, when the fetus's major organ systems are laid down, and to initiate, or resume, therapy in the fourth month. The important thing is that women get all the available information and that they, and not their health care providers, be the ones to make such decisions.

Occupational Health

Many of the issues we have been considering are relevant to the health needs of women in the workplace. American physicians do not pay sufficient attention to occupational health and, since women are looked on as wives and mothers rather than as workers, women's occupational health gets even less attention than men's.

To the extent that women's participation in the workforce is recognized, their health needs tend not to be differentiated from those of men. But the health concerns of female and male workers are not identical, since they tend to do different work and thus be exposed to different health risks.

Women are employed mostly as office, hospital, or child care workers, waitresses, teachers, and cleaners, as well as on assembly lines in food processing and clothing manufacturing, and in microelectronics. They often do piece-work rather than receive an hourly wage, and their work tends to be repetitive and to require fast speeds. Much of it must be done standing or sitting for many hours in the same position, while going through the same movements over and over again. To the extent that a job involves interaction with children or sick people, workers are exposed to infections, and many women work in situations where they are expected always to be courteous and cheerful.

In addition, women's work is often temporary, part-time, of low prestige, and poorly paid; and it is rarely unionized, so that workers are on their own in negotiations with their employers. Women workers also are often exposed to suggestive "teasing," "jokes," and outright sexual harassment or coercion

99

from their colleagues or superiors.

Where women have entered workplaces that used to hire only men, the work situations have evolved around physical, psychological, and social attributes of men, which can differ in significant ways from those of women. One does not have to believe that "biology is destiny" to acknowledge that in most contemporary societies women are, on average, smaller, lighter, and physically less strong than men and that women carry a greater domestic workload than men do even when both have full-time jobs. The psychological, social, and physical demands of any job on women therefore are quite different from those on men. Sometimes women also menstruate and get pregnant and at such times their health needs may be different than at other times and than the needs of men. That is nothing to be self-conscious about; it is a fact of life which a society that values its members in all their diversity must recognize and accommodate.

Writing in the July 1994 issue of the *Women's Review of Books*, Karen Messing, a Canadian biologist and expert on occupational health, points out that women's working conditions are understudied on the false assumption that women's work is less hazardous than men's. True, women's jobs often do not involve risks of severe accidents, but that does not mean that they do not involve hazards to health. Women's work is physically and emotionally stressful and often injures muscles, tendons, and joints.

Despite the myth that women work for pocket money, most women, like men, need their job to pay the bills. Yet, there has been no study on the health effects of involuntary part-time status or of intermittent or irregular work on the health of women workers. Messing has pointed out that the effects of unemployment on health have been studied among the wives of male workers while studying these effects among the men themselves, but not among women workers, even though research has shown that between ages 25 and 45 women workers are more likely to be out of a job than men.

As might be expected, the subject of reproductive hazards in the workplace is steeped in ideology. Men's role in procreation has been ignored, so that scientists have only recently begun to look systematically at the effects toxic chemicals and radiation have on the quality and quantity of sperm. By contrast, unless they were willing to be surgically sterilized, women of reproductive age (interpreted as ages 16 to 54) have been denied high-paying jobs, traditionally held by men, in the automotive and other industries on the grounds that the work might endanger a "potential" fetus. Fortunately, the U.S. Supreme Court ruled this practice illegal in 1991. Women also have had to go to court to establish the right to remain in their jobs or be transferred, at equal pay, during pregnancy or when they return to work after giving birth.

As with AIDS, the concern has not been for the women themselves, but for the health of the mythic fetus women are thought to harbor in their bodies at all times. And it certainly does not extend to women who work in traditional women's jobs as nurses, X-ray technologists, or laboratory technicians, or as cleaning women in surgical operating rooms, scientific laboratories, or the chemical or biotechnology industry. Nor are beauticians, secretaries, workers in the ceramics industry, or domestic workers (in a word, just about all women) warned about the hazards of their work to their own health or to that of a fetus, should they be pregnant. In reality, concerns about the effects of toxic chemicals and radiation are being used to keep women out of jobs from which they were previously excluded by discriminatory employment practices, while most working women or men are not protected against occupational hazards to health.

Nor can the courts be relied on for help. Twelve years after the U.S. Congress passed the Civil Rights Act of 1964, which outlawed discrimination on the basis of race or sex, a majority of the Supreme Court decided that the General Electric Company's exclusion of health coverage for pregnancy-related disabilities did not discriminate against women, even though male workers were covered for disabilities that affect only men (*General Electric Company v. Gilbert*, 1976). The dissenting minority pointed out that the Court, in effect, ruled that the company's health plan was consistent with civil rights law because men as well as women were excluded from coverage for health problems related to pregnancy, and women as well as men were covered for prostate surgery.

This may be an extreme example, but I hope I have convinced you that the disregard for women's health in many facets of our lives, as well as the exaggerated concern in some, are not based on considerations for the health needs of women, children, or indeed men and that they are detrimental to people's health and welfare.

Sexism and Sociobiology

For Our Own Good and the Good of the Species

During the last third of the nineteenth century, as of the twentieth, defenders of male prerogatives in the marketplace and the home have felt threatened by women's demands for equality. The agendas of the movement for women's rights in these two periods have been different and so have the responses. In the 1800s, the movement focused on access to education and the professions, birth control, and the vote. The current focus has been on equal rights (the ERA), reproductive rights, the right to exercise sexual and affectional preferences, and the economic struggle for equal pay for equal work or, more recently, equal pay for work of comparable value. During both periods, distinguished academics, including Harvard professors, have provided arguments to support the status quo. Both times, the arguments have been neither new nor convincing but, because of Harvard's prestige, they have been announced with greater fanfare and have gained a wider hearing than they merited.

Brains or Ovaries

As girls gained access to education, it became clear that girls' brains were up to the task. Women's colleges opened and attracted successful students, as did adventurous coeducational colleges and universities. By the 1860s and 1870s, scientific arguments about the inferiority of women's brains were no longer acceptable in most quarters. The question of the day was no longer: can women do it? New reasons were required to restrict women's access to higher education and the professions. The question became: is it good for them? And who could answer this better than physicians, scientifically trained men, who had been caring for the health of women?

The times were problematic for "regular" physicians—that is, the men who had been able to go to Europe for their medical training or to the few U.S. medical schools that were beginning to model themselves on the European schools. Women were prominent among "irregular" healers where husband-wife teams were not unusual. Most midwives were women, and women had always cared for the ill at home. So, when women began to apply to the medical schools where the "regulars" were being trained, male physicians had reason to worry that becoming a physician might look like a natural extension of work women had been doing all along. What is more, the prevailing modesty of upper-class women was likely to make many of them prefer to be seen by a woman physician if they had a choice, and in this they would have their husbands' approval. Physicians therefore viewed the entry of women into the medical profession as an economic threat, particularly at a time when, rightly or wrongly, they had begun to believe that the profession was already overpopulated.[1] For all these reasons medical school students and practicing physicians did not look with favor on women's attempts to enter their profession. So, forward came physicians to explain that it would be detrimental to women's health to become physicians.

Foremost among them was Dr. Edward H. Clarke, who held the chair of *materia medica* at Harvard Medical School from 1855 to 1872, when he resigned his professorship and became a member of Harvard's Board of Overseers. In 1869, Clarke wrote an article for the *Boston Medical and Surgical Journal* in which he argued that women had a right "to every function and opportunity which our planet offers, that man has," if they are equal to it, but he warned against undue haste: "Let the experiment...be fairly made...[and] in 50 years we shall get the answer."[2]

However, Clarke soon turned against the notion that women should enjoy these opportunities together with men. Let women be educated to the best of their capabilities, but separately. Of course, even if women wanted to take Clarke up on his "experiment," they could not follow his advice because the only medical schools that existed at the time were operated by and for men. So women kept applying to those medical schools, and even to Clarke's own institution, Harvard Medical School. Under this threat, Clarke drew back from his proposed experiment and in an address to the New England Women's Club of Boston, delivered in 1872, he put forward arguments that were published the next year as *Sex in Education; or, A Fair Chance for the Girls.*[3] This book went through seventeen editions in the next thirteen years and a bookseller in Ann Arbor, who claimed to have sold two hundred copies in one day, remarked that "the book bids fair to nip coeducation in the bud."[4]

In the introduction, Clarke stressed that the point is not that one sex is superior to the other, but that they are different, and on this he based his assertion that coeducation is detrimental to women's health. A girl obviously can go to school and do whatever a boy can do. "But it is not true that she can do all this, and retain uninjured health and a future secured from neuralgia, uterine disease, hysteria, and other derangements of the nervous system, if she follows the same method that boys are trained in."[5] And if this was not sufficiently convincing, he offered a pithier slogan: "The physiological motto is, Educate a man for manhood, a woman for womanhood, both for humanity. In this lies the hope of the race."[6]

The rest of the book was built around this "physiological" rallying cry. In the chapter entitled "Chiefly Physiological," Clarke described in painful detail all the ways women's physiology would be injured if girls were educated the same as boys and therefore developed their brains rather than pay due regard to developing their menstrual functions. "The organization of the male grows steadily, gradually and equally, from birth to maturity," he stated authoritatively, whereas girls must pass through a critical transition when they must "allow a sufficient opportunity for the establishment of their periodical functions.... Moreover, unless the work is accomplished at that period, unless the reproductive mechanism is built and put in good working order at that time, it is never perfectly accomplished afterwards."[7] And it is not enough for girls to exercise care in how they *begin* to menstruate. "'Precautions should be...repeated...again and again, until at length the *habit* of regular, healthy menstruation is established'" wrote Clarke, attributing this piece of wisdom to "the accomplished London physician, and lecturer on diseases of women," Dr. Charles West.[8] And Clarke went on: "There have been instances, and I have seen such, of females in whom the special mechanism we are speaking of remained germinal—undeveloped.... They graduated from school or college excellent scholars, but with undeveloped ovaries. Later they married, and were sterile."[9]

Here Clarke was speaking to another fear of the time, for the cry had gone up that the native-born upper classes were not reproducing themselves, whereas poor, immigrant families were having too many children. Therefore the possibility that education would render upper-class women sterile was something to alarm both women and men of his class.

I have quoted Clarke at such length not just because I like his authoritative voice, but because I want readers to see the ways he transformed prejudices of his time and class into scientific truths. Rather than go on and quote from the so-called case histories that Clarke cited in his next chapter, entitled "Chiefly Clinical," some of which were quickly shown to be inventions,[10] I want to point out that, of course, Clarke did not go unchallenged. The abolitionist Thomas Wentworth Higginson (Emily Dickinson's friend and correspondent) pointed out that Clarke's dire descriptions meant little as long as he offered no comparable information about how education affected the health of boys. Other critics objected that his proposal that girls' education be coordinated with the demands of their menstrual cycles was equivalent to no schooling for girls, since an entire classroom of girl students does not menstruate in synchrony. And what of the teacher, wondered Eliza B. Duffey: "She too requires her regular furlough, and then what are the scholars to do?"[11] Duffey further asked whether Clarke wished to suggest that wives and mothers also require three- to four-day menstrual furloughs each month.

Despite Clarke's best efforts, women gradually gained access to medical schools. But the doors of Harvard Medical School remained sealed until late in World War II, when economic considerations and a decline in the quality of male applicants induced this last medical bastion of sex discrimination to admit twelve women to the class that entered in the fall of 1945. Yet, even at that late date, in the debate preceding the vote some faculty members argued that their colleagues who were planning to admit women were ignoring "the fundamental biological law that the primary function of women is to bear and raise children."[12]

Of Eggs and Human Nature

Let us now move to the 1970s when the present wave of the women's movement was becoming a significant political force. As might be expected, again scientists rose to the challenge and pointed out that the status quo was in tune with nature. And since this is a Harvard story, I will concentrate on the contributions of another Harvard professor, the biologist Edward O. Wilson, a member of Harvard's elite Society of Fellows and a popular teacher.

Wilson's research has been concerned with the

classification and behavior of ants. Therefore, it came as no surprise when in 1971 Harvard University Press published his handsomely illustrated *The Insect Societies*. However, this was followed in 1975 by the publication of another book with the more ambitious title *Sociobiology: The New Synthesis*. It is rare for a scientific text of 697 pages, which includes a 22-page glossary and 64 pages of bibliography, to become a media event or to sell over 100,000 copies despite its $25 cover price and its awkward ten-by-ten-inch format, that makes it too large to fit into most bookshelves. Yet, with careful nurturing by the Harvard University Press, including talk shows, cocktail parties, write-ups in *Time* and *Newsweek*, and a rave review in the widely read *Atlantic Monthly* by Fred Hapgood, at the time a writer for the Harvard University Publicity Office, this book propelled Wilson to instant fame. The subsequent publication of *On Human Nature* in 1978 stirred hardly a ripple among Wilson's scientific colleagues but garnered a Pulitzer Prize for literature.

What is all this about and how does it relate to the way scientists have used their purportedly objective expertise to support the status quo against women's striving for equality? Before examining Wilson's sociobiological arguments in greater detail, I want to make clear that sexism lies at the center of sociobiology because of the way sociobiologists deal with the concept of "reproductive success." Following Darwin, reproductive success is measured by the number of offspring an individual produces who themselves grow up and reproduce. This brings us up against an asymmetry between females and males that arises from two facts: (1) that in many species males can produce far greater numbers of sperm in a lifetime than females can produce eggs, and (2) that eggs are usually larger than sperm. Sociobiologists take these two innocent-looking differences to mean that a female, by definition, has a larger "investment" in each of her eggs than a male has in each of his sperm. And since each individual is said to be trying to maximize the number of her or his genetic offspring, this asymmetry in size and number of reproductive cells is taken to imply that females are "by nature" more protective of their offspring than are males, since females cannot produce as many.

Many things are wrong with this line of argument. First of all, it is a metaphor, and a questionable one at that, to speak of eggs and sperm as investments. Females form eggs as part of their metabolism as do males sperm, and it takes no more effort or energy to produce one than the other. Our muscle cells cannot be said to represent more of an investment or to cost us more, and hence be more precious to us, than our liver cells merely because they are larger or because we have more of them. We need both, and these kinds of comparisons between them are meaningless. Secondly, since it takes only one sperm to fertilize an egg, no more sperm can become adults than can eggs. And since the males of most species do not divide into wimps and superstuds, in any given species or population about as many males as females get to have offspring and in about equal numbers.

Yet Wilson and other sociobiologists use this purported asymmetry in the reproductive investments of women and men to account for *the* division of labor (as though there were only one) as described, for example, by the statement that in "an American industrial city, no less than [in] a band of hunter-gatherers...women and children remain in the residential area while men forage for game or its symbolic equivalent in the form of barter and money."[13] This statement obscures the fact that there is no unique or universal division of labor. It also ignores that among hunter-gatherers, women do the major share of foraging, that in numerous African and Latin American societies the markets, where bartering and the exchange of money happen, are women's domain, and that most women in our own society do not get the chance to stay home "in the residential area" and care for their children, even if they want to, because they need to earn money. Yet Wilson takes the purported asymmetry in "reproductive investments" to justify the prediction he published in the *New York Times Magazine* that "even with identical education and equal access to all professions, men are likely to play a disproportionate role in political life, business, and science."[14] (Indeed, he was apparently so impressed with this prediction that he repeated it, slightly reworded, in *On Human Nature*.[15]) A further example of how literally Wilson takes the investment metaphor of reproduction is his amazingly inappropriate appraisal of female prostitution: "It is to be expected that prostitutes are the despised members of society; they have abandoned their valuable reproductive investments to strangers."[16] Erased are the social conditions under which the system of prostitution operates in our society—the pimps, corrupt police, drug dealers, junkies, teenage runaways, women trying to support children on more than a minimum wage, men buying sex they cannot get any other way, and so on. Prostitutes are neglectful people who squander their investments and do not clip coupons!

Wilson defines sociobiology as "the systematic study of the biological basis of all social behavior" and promises that his synthesis will come to include "sociology and the other social sciences, as well as the humanities...[as] the last branches of biology."[17]

He asserts that the basic elements of human nature can be identified by means of an elaboration of Darwin's theory of evolution through natural selection, expanded to include the twentieth-century concept of "genetic fitness." This concept involves the assumption that those traits come to be inherited that are "adaptive." The argument runs as follows: individuals who carry genes "for" adaptive traits leave more descendants than other individuals do, so that in future generations the genes concerned with these traits outnumber the genes involved with less adaptive traits. When it comes to behavior, sociobiologists argue that this means we do things that are good for our own survival and reproduction so that the genes that have made us behave that way in the first place will be spread to future generations.

The kinds of behaviors that Wilson identifies as adaptive—hence as basic components of human nature—are aggression, territoriality, selfishness, and the tendency to establish dominance hierarchies; the various secondary sexual behaviors, such as fondling and kissing, that make relationships between women and men emotionally satisfying; altruistic behaviors that accrue also to one's own benefit; and religious-spiritual traits, such as the need to believe in something beyond oneself. "The predisposition to religious belief," he writes, "is the most complex and powerful force in the human mind and in all probability an ineradicable part of human nature."[18] Yet, "[a]lthough the manifestations of the religious experience are resplendent and multidimensional, and so complicated that the finest of psychoanalysts and philosophers get lost in their labyrinth, I believe that religious practices can be mapped onto the dimensions of genetic advantage and evolutionary change."[19] And, of course, included among adaptive behaviors are men's "predisposition" to dominate women and women's greater contribution than men's to child care. "Because [the egg] represents a considerable energetic investment on the part of the mother the embryo is often sequestered and protected, and sometimes its care is extended into the postnatal period. *This is the reason why parental care is normally provided by the female....*" (my italics).[20]

But these are by no means the only behaviors for which Wilson postulates genetic components ("behavioral genes"). Included, among others, are homosexuality, schizophrenia (or rather, "a major part of the tendency to become schizophrenic,"[21] whatever that means), and the incest taboo—that is, the avoidance of incestuous behavior. (Apparently Wilson is unaware of the literature documenting the widespread occurrence of father-daughter, brother-sister, and even grandfather-granddaughter incest at all levels of our society.)

Of course, Wilson recognizes that much of human social behavior is cultural but, like other sociobiologists, he believes that he can identify the genetic components of behavior by identifying its adaptive components. They constitute that "stubborn" kernel of human nature that "cannot be forced without cost."[22] He states that "the great majority of human societies have evolved toward sexual domination as though sliding along a rachet"[23] and warns that although we are sufficiently flexible to make change possible, "the early predispositions that characterize sex would have to be blunted" and "regulations" would be "required" that "would certainly place some freedoms in jeopardy."[24]

Wilson leaves out or at least underplays the fact that a crucial characteristic of humans, one of the things that sets us apart, is our enormous adaptability, our capacity to occupy, use effectively, and thereby reshape just about all environments and to endow them with special significance in the effort to survive and to give meaning to our survival. It is highly questionable whether it means anything to speak of "human nature" apart from the ways people function in societies and cultures. Yet the sweep of Wilson's generalizations extends from termites to rhesus monkeys to humans, and draws analogies between human societies that are widely separated in time and space and in their cultural, economic, and political contents. He excuses this by saying that rather than dwell on "details...it is the parallelism in the major features...that demands our closest attention."[25] But what he takes to be "detail" or a "major feature" is of course influenced by what he is trying to prove.

A crucial methodological problem in human sociobiology is that it is impossible to prove that adaptive behaviors are inherited biologically and handed on through cultural learning. We transform our cultural and natural environments all the while they transform us. To sort genetic from environmental contributions to traits, one must be able to specify and quantify the trait and completely control the organism's genetic make-up and environment. This can be done only for a few traits of organisms that can be grown under carefully monitored laboratory conditions. It is, of course, impossible to use this method with people. To overcome this difficulty, Wilson and other sociobiologists argue that if they can show that a trait occurs in different societies and, perhaps, also among some animals, this suggests that it is adaptive and has been established through natural selection, and therefore has become genetic.

This line of reasoning is misleading for many reasons. The most important one is that organisms that look or act alike need not do so for the same evolutionary or genetic reasons. This is why biologists usually are careful to distinguish between what they call "analogies" and "homologies." Analogous traits fulfill a similar function and may look similar, but have different evolutionary origins. Examples are the wings of insects, birds, and bats, or the eyes of lobsters, squids, and humans. Homologous traits are traits that have had a common evolutionary history and often fulfill similar kinds of functions, although their evolutionary paths may have diverged so that they may not look alike. Examples are the hairs and horns of mammals, or reptilian scales and birds' feathers. Paleontologists who track evolutionary lines spend much time and care scanning the fossil record so as to distinguish homologies from analogies, since the latter are useless for establishing evolutionary and genetic relationships.

Clearly, behavioral traits cannot be analyzed in this way. Therefore, it is impossible to prove that similar behaviors, though perhaps adaptive, are not merely analogous solutions to similar or indeed common problems—how to fly, how to fend off intruders, how to share tasks that need to get done. Observations of behavioral similarities do not permit one to deduce the existence of "behavioral genes." Nor does it clarify the situation to suggest, as Wilson does, that perhaps genes control not behavior, but "tendencies" or "predispositions" to behave in certain ways. For example, he writes:

> [It is] possible, and in my judgment even proba-
> ble, that the positions of genes having indirect
> effects on the most complex forms of behavior
> will soon be mapped on the human chromo-
> somes. These genes are unlikely to prescribe
> particular patterns of behavior; there will be no
> mutations for a particular sexual practice or
> mode of dress. The behavioral genes more prob-
> ably influence the ranges of the form and inten-
> sity of emotional responses, the thresholds of
> arousals, the readiness to learn certain stimuli
> as opposed to others, and the pattern of sensi-
> tivity to additional environmental factors that
> point cultural evolution in one direction as
> opposed to another.[26]

Such assertions are so inclusive and vague that they are meaningless. They certainly cannot be proved scientifically. (What sensitivities, emotions, arousals, stimuli? What does it mean to "point cul-tural evolution in [a] direction?") The impossibility of distinguishing behavioral analogies from homologies, the many levels of interaction between different genes, the many unknown events that intervene between the functions of genes and observable behaviors, and the complexity of the mutual transformations among organisms and their environments all force me to conclude that Wilson's aim to develop an accurate picture of the evolutionary, hence genetic, basis of social behavior, can probably not be realized for animals, and surely not for people. Some of the necessary measurements cannot even be conceptualized, and of those we can specify, most cannot be carried out. How can one hope either to prove or disprove claims of "innate predispositions" for such ill-defined and culturally variable behavioral traits as dominance, aggression, maternalism, or selfishness? The inherent difficulties of precisely specifying and assigning these kinds of characterizations make it easy to compose stories from which to draw conclusions that are in line with one's preconceptions.

What Wilson perceives to be "human nature," and what he therefore explicates biologically, is in its essential features a stereotyped description of how things are in capitalist countries, with their divisions of sex, race, and class that determine great differences in the power people have over their own and other people's lives. To make the evolutionary argument, he tries to show that this stereotype also characterizes other societies—human and animal—that are organized quite differently. This leads to an enormously confusing use of concepts such as dominance or aggression, and confounds any effort to understand how divisions of labor affect roles and power and to explain the origins of observed differences in social, economic, and political status between women and men.

Assertions such as that men dominate women in all societies conceal more than they reveal until we know how "dominance" is defined. The argument for the universality of male dominance is usually based on the fact that all societies have divisions of labor. When we are told that in many of them men's tasks are valued more highly than women's, these valuations can easily be in the eye of the anthropologist-beholder. For example, for egalitarian societies, such as some of the hunter-gatherer peoples in Africa, it may be quite wrong to try to fit their divisions of roles into the power differentials that are implicit in the concept of dominance hierarchies.

We in the industrialized countries have grown up in hierarchically structured societies, so that, to us, dominance hierarchies appear natural and inevitable. But it is a mistake to apply the same categories to societies that function quite differently and to pretend that differences between our society and theirs can be expressed merely as matters of degree. What I am saying is that one cannot rate apples, oranges, and pears on their "appleness." They are not more or less like apples; they are *different*.

To take widely different and complex social manifestations and scale them along one dimension does violence to the sources and significance of human social behavior. Western technological societies have developed in their ways for their own historical reasons. Other societies have their histories that have led them to their social forms. To try and classify these cultures into categories derived from the way our society operates today ignores our history and their histories. To take people who live on islands, in plains, or on high mountain ranges, between the Arctic zones and the tropics, in industrial cities and towns or in agricultural communities, and pretend that one can identify and analyze the basic features of their societies by reading and thinking about them, rather than that one needs to experience their diversities, is typical of Western ethnocentrism.

When it comes to comparing cultures the world over with those of Europe and the United States, another problem arises from the fact that every other place on Earth has been affected by what has happened in the industrialized countries. David Livingstone's accounts express his shock at the power women exerted in the "petticoat governments" (his expression) with which he had to deal in Africa. And there are comparable reports from early Europeans arriving on the American continent. Euro-American traders, missionaries, and governments have affected customs, economic arrangements, and politics in all parts of the world. If we find similarities between Western practices and those of peoples who appear to be culturally as well as geographically distant from us, we must consider the possibility that Westerners put them there.

Wither Veritas?

Let me be clear: we are people and not monkeys or ants. Furthermore, each of us is unique. Genes have something to do with our humanity and with our individual differences, but we cannot know how much they have to do with them. When something cannot be proved, yet the pretense that it can be or has been proved is used to argue for or against social policies and forms of government (Wilson tells us that Marxism is "based on an inaccurate interpretation of human nature"[27]), the effort is not a quest for knowledge. It is a political campaign.

Writing about the problems inherent in doing scientific research on questions that are central to the ways our society is organized, the Brown University biologist Anne Fausto-Sterling points out that to do science as objectively as we can, we must try to be aware of the many facets of our subjectivity that are likely to affect the way we view the area of our inquiry.[28] When it comes to sex differences, it is questionable whether anyone can hold opinions, or do research, that express anything other than her or his beliefs about how society operates, or should operate, because everything about our lives, including our language, is gendered. In as loaded and value-laden an area as sex differences, everything becomes political, a way of persuading others to promote what we believe to be correct ways for the society to function. Under these circumstances, it is wrong to ignore, or even deny, one's biases and pretend that one is doing objective research or dispensing objective information.

When Edward Clarke wraps himself in the mantle of medical authority to mouth the prejudices of the men of his class, that is deception. When Edward Wilson opens the last chapter of *Sociobiology: The New Synthesis* with the words "Let us now consider man [sic] in the free spirit of natural history, as though we were zoologists from another planet completing a catalog of social species on Earth,"[29] that too is deception. He is not an observer from another planet. He is a Harvard professor and a scientist, with group and personal interests. To pretend scientific detachment when words are as suffused with social values as are the languages of medicine and sociobiology, is naive or malicious. Even Harvard professors need to face the fact that they cannot live outside the political concerns of their time and that some areas of life are so steeped in politics—and sex is one of them—that objectivity becomes synonymous with unacknowledged partisanship.

Some forty years ago, Margaret Mead pointed out that, although different societies have different and often opposite divisions of labor by sex, no matter how work is shared out—whether women or men carry the heaviest loads, whether women or men go to market—each society believes its way of doing things is inevitable and natural.[30] In our society, in which scientific experts interpret nature for us, physicians and scientists are the ones to assure us that our division of labor reflects biological imperatives. And when they come wrapped in the mantle of Harvard's motto "Veritas," who would dare not to believe them?

Which Facts?
Whose Life?

A review of *The Facts of Life: Science and the Abortion Controversy.* By Harold J. Morowitz and James S. Trefil. Oxford University Press, 1992. Pp. 179. $19.95.

The anthropologist Rayna Rapp opens a recent article about women's experiences of amniocentesis with this excerpt from an interview with a 39-year-old New York woman: "When we walked into the doctor's office, both my husband and I were crying. [The doctor] looked up and said, 'What's wrong? Why are you in tears?' 'It's the baby, the baby is going to die,' I said. 'That isn't a baby,' he said firmly. 'It's a collection of cells that made a mistake.'"[1]

Clearly, there is a wide divergence in the ways different people perceive pregnancy and its termination. In the abortion debate, opinions range from total support for a woman's right to decide whether to abort, and when, to total interdiction. Even among advocates of abortion rights opinions differ. In the heady days of women's liberation some twenty-five years ago, feminists argued that unless women can avoid unwanted births, we are not free to participate fully in heterosexual relationships. Over the years, the link between abortion and sexuality has been pushed into the closet. Support for abortion rights increasingly focuses on women's need to plan their families and to terminate pregnancies resulting from rape or incest.

Different groups draw the line at different stages of pregnancy, though in the United States most abortion rights advocates support the distinction the Supreme Court established in 1973 in *Roe v. Wade*. This ruling holds that, during the first two trimesters, abortion is a private matter to be decided by a woman in consultation with her physician. Only in the third trimester, when a fetus can survive outside a woman's womb, may the state regulate abortions, though it need not do so. Increasingly, women's rights activists have accepted *Roe*'s concerns with privacy and choice, and abandoned the issue of sexual liberation.

In the twenty years since *Roe*, abortion rights have been narrowed by legislatures and the courts. For example, states or the federal government need not pay for abortions of poor women receiving social insurance (medicaid) or of insured government workers, including women in the military and female dependents of military men. Various states have imposed a requirement that minors obtain parental consent, in some states by both parents even if they live apart. A regulation introduced by the Bush administration even provided that, in family planning clinics or related services which receive federal funding, no one other than a physician may mention abortion to clients. While this absurd regulation has been repealed, nonetheless it has become increasingly difficult for poor women and for young women without supportive parents to obtain abortions.

Perhaps the most drastic changes in the conditions under which women who need abortions, and clinics that provide them, must operate have resulted from direct confrontations by abortion opponents. But here, too, we must distinguish among different views. Some pacifist and religious groups oppose abortion because they oppose killing human beings, and perhaps also animals, under any circumstances. They represent a tiny fraction of that minority among Americans which opposes abortion. The Catholic church holds that life begins at conception and therefore opposes abortion as murder, although it does not oppose other forms of killing, such as wars or the death penalty. (Incidentally, Catholics have proportionally as many abortions as do women from other religious denominations.) Differences also exist among anti-abortion activists in the New Right. Some groups, usually led by women, focus on women's "natural" mission as mothers. They lead prayers and vigils, and hail women who decide not to abort despite hardships. By constrast, "Operation Rescue" is male-led and tries to intimidate clients, physicians, and other clinic personnel and to do whatever it takes to close clinics down.

In the abortion debate, the radical right conceals its anti-feminist agenda of controlling women's lives and especially women's sexuality by championing "the unborn." This obscures the fact that "the unborn" develops within the body of a woman, a human being who may have needs and intentions that do not include having a baby at that stage in her life, or perhaps ever.

The authors of *The Facts of Life* try to ground the abortion debate in modern science. Yet, by focusing on the biology of fertilization and embryonic development, they too leave women out of account. The dilemma they confront is that, as scientists, they acknowledge that a developing fetus is both alive and human. Yet, like most Americans, they support abortion rights up to a point. They solve this conundrum by deciding that, biologically, a fetus is more animal than human until it develops what they call "humanness." And, as they point out, though killing animals may be frowned on, it is not murder. On the basis of a mixture of evolutionary and embryological arguments, they then conclude that humanness is attained when the cerebral cortex becomes recognizably human around twenty-four weeks of gestation. Though they write with admirable clarity, the argument reads more like a Scholastic treatise about "ensoulment" than like the "objective" science they claim it represents.

The authors assert that specifying humanness provides a scientific way to resolve the abortion question, but this solution is laden with problems. The central one is that they ignore that their scientific views are embedded in cultural beliefs. Many differences, and similarities, exist between humans and other animals. Privileging the brain is not "scientific," but is grounded in the mind/body split that dominates our culture. And there is no scientific reason why killing animals is permissible, when killing humans is not. The distinction does not originate in biology or evolution, but is part of the Judeo-Christian tradition in which Jehovah gave humans dominion over the remainder of creation. (For further discussions of this issue, see the forthcoming book, edited by Lynda Birke and Ruth Hubbard, *Reinventing Biology: Respect for Life and the Creation of Knowledge*, Indiana University Press, 1995.) Buddhism and other traditions do not accept it.

Which Facts? Whose Life?

Finally, the authors finesse a question that is central to the abortion debate when they mention in passing, and without comment, that taking a human life is murder only when it is done "without the sanction of the state." This caveat raises the question of why the state should forbid abortion when it sanctions killing persons convicted of certain crimes, glorifies killing in wartime, and permits it in self-defense. Indeed, why is not terminating an unwanted pregnancy a form of self-defense by women?

Because of their exclusive focus on "the fetus," the authors ignore that, whatever the law says, as long as there are unwanted pregnancies there will be abortions. The significant question is whether abortions are legal and safe, or illegal and likely to damage or kill women. Where abortion is legal, it involves fewer risks for women than a full-term birth does. An "objective" book about abortion should consider the impacts gestation, birth, and abortion have on women. Scientific information about these topics bears on political decisions about abortion, but this book omits such "facts of life."

The Politics of Fetal/Maternal Conflict

There are all kinds of ways in which societies interpret women's procreative abilities and use these interpretations to structure and define our participation in society. Hence, women's ability to gestate and birth children is used to control our behavior somewhat differently in the United States from the ways fecundity and procreation are used to control women in some other societies. The new procreative technologies and the anti-abortion movement have something to do with what is happening in the United States but so do other social forces.

One way to begin to explore this situation is to look at the way Americans view pregnancy in this final decade of the twentieth century. Here, two trends reinforce each other. First, there is the image of the disembodied embryo or fetus, floating somewhere in space. This is illustrated by a NOVA television program called "How Are Babies Made?" The program opens with a gowned male doctor handing a newborn to a gowned nurse who, of course, is female. The rest of the program is about eggs, sperm, cell nuclei, early and later stages of embryonic development, and the developing fetus. At one point, we get to see a piece of the placenta. That famous visitor from outer space would have no way to gather from this presentation that everything shown in the film happens inside the body of a woman. Women and pregnancy are never mentioned. All we hear about are the mythic embryo and fetus.

Now let us look at the changing image of mothers. In her book *Recreating Motherhood*, Barbara Katz Rothman (1989) looked at the transformations in the image of the mother in popular culture as we go from the 1950s and '60s to the 1970s and '80s. Throughout these decades mothers have always been portrayed as bad for their children, but their ways of being bad have changed. In the 1950s and '60s, mothers damaged their children by being too self-sacrificing, like Portnoy's mother. But in the 1970s and '80s, the smothering mother was replaced by the selfish mother, the woman out to fulfill herself at the expense of her child. The new prototype is the mother portrayed in the film *Kramer vs. Kramer*, the self-absorbed woman who abandons her child to the tender mercies of its father.

Putting together the disembodied embryo and the selfish mother, you readily get the three practices I want us to think about:

1. criminal prosecutions of women for endangering the fetus within their bodies,

2. court-mandated Caesarean sections, and

3. fetal protection as grounds for excluding women from jobs with relatively good pay and health and retirement benefits, which have previously been held only by men and to which women have recently begun to gain access.

All three of these practices produce media stories that strengthen the cultural image of neglectful women putting their fetuses at risk. And although these particular practices demonize primarily poor or working-class women, the aura they create can be used to control the behavior of middle- and upper-class women as well. After all, different kinds of "experts" are always ready to make middle- and upper-class women feel guilty for putting their own career needs ahead of the needs of their future or present children. Middle- and upper-class American women may be spared accusations of fetal abuse, but they are frequently accused of neglecting their maternal duties when they postpone childbearing or when they delegate the care of their children to others (including the fathers of those children). Meanwhile, in the United States, in contrast to several other industrialized nations, there is no public responsibility either for childcare or for adequate nutrition and healthcare for pregnant women. Women get blamed, but there are few places where they can go for help.

Criminal Prosecutions

Numerous women—most of them poor, many of them battered—have been jailed for drinking alcohol or using drugs while pregnant. How do the authorities find out about them? In one case, because a battered women's shelter brought a pregnant woman to the hospital for treatment of her bruises. A blood test revealed alcohol, and promptly she was charged with "felony child abuse."

A case still being litigated in Massachusetts involves Josephine Pellegrini of Brockton who in

1989 gave birth in a public hospital. The newborn was healthy, but a routine blood test showed traces of cocaine in its blood. The Commonwealth promptly charged Pellegrini with distributing cocaine to a minor via the umbilical cord and also with possession of an illegal substance (McNamara, 1989). The "distributing" charge, which carries a minimum sentence of three years in state prison, was dismissed in 1992, since in Massachusetts a fetus does not have legal standing as a minor, but in March 1993 the Supreme Judicial Court upheld the "possession" charge. A legal issue that remains to be decided is whether the mandatory reporting statute, under which anyone who suspects child neglect or abuse must report the situation, can be used to prosecute someone for the harm that person may be doing to her/himself when there is no evidence that she or he has, in fact, harmed the child whom this statute is intended to protect.

Another legal issue, raised in a review by Kary Moss (1990), is that administering drug tests to an infant without the parent's consent violates parental rights. As Moss points out, "A positive toxicology [drug test] alone does not provide substantive information about the impairment of mother or child.... It does not measure frequency of drug use, but says only that a drug was introduced in the last 24 to 72 hours." There is also the social and medical problem that using the mandatory reporting statute this way is likely to deter pregnant women from consulting drug counselors or other providers of health or social services for fear that it will lead to criminal prosecution and so deprive mothers of custody and terminate their parental rights. Linking the health care or social service system with legal prosecutions erodes women's often tenuous trust of service providers and may, in fact, imperil the health of women, fetuses, and newborns.

Eventually, most charges of delivering drugs to fetuses in utero have been dismissed, either on technical grounds or because a fetus is not a person. As a result, state prosecutors are formulating ever more ingenious charges, such as, for example, the "possession" charge against Josephine Pellegrini. In another case, Jennifer Johnson, a woman in Florida, was convicted of a felony for passing cocaine, this time not to her fetus but to her newborn in the moments before the umbilical cord was cut *(Florida v. Johnson,* 1989). Johnson's sentence included the proviso that she get drug treatment (which she had tried to get) and gainful employment (which she had tried to find), and that she not use drugs or associate with anyone who does, drink any alcohol, or enter a bar as conditions of her parole (though no provisions were made to help her move out of her neighborhood). In other words, although she tried, and was unable, to get the services she needed to stop using drugs, she was punished for not having gotten them.

Let us take a closer look at what this is about. I suppose most people would agree that it is not a good thing for pregnant women to drink excessive amounts of alcohol or to smoke or use drugs. But if the state wants to protect a fetus, the way to do that is to make it possible for pregnant women—and women in general—to have access to proper housing, food, jobs, a decent living environment, and good prenatal care. Quite the contrary, since 1980 resources available to poor women have been diminishing. Health and nutrition programs for women and children have been slashed, not to speak of jobs and housing. Though overall infant mortality has declined during this century, infant mortality in this country now is twice as high for African-American as for Euro-American infants, the same as it was a hundred years ago (Hogue and Hargraves, 1993).

The so-called war on drugs has produced a situation in which a single blood test on a pregnant woman or a newborn is sufficient to label that woman a drug abuser and call in the state. Courts increasingly are criminalizing poor women for behaving in ways that could endanger their fetus, irrespective of whether their babies can be shown to have sustained damage. There need be no symptoms or other indications that the baby has been mistreated in any way. This way of implicating drug abuse often results in misdiagnoses and mislabeling (Moss, 1990). For example, on the basis of a blood test on a newborn, in 1990 Cambridge Hospital accused a young, unmarried, African-American woman of having used drugs while pregnant. The woman and her mother denied the charge and sought legal help. Further tests indicated that the chemicals which were detected in the baby's bloodstream had been administered to the woman by her medical attendants during labor.

The mandatory reporting policy can wreak havoc with the lives of women and children, and more so the more vulnerable the women are. A poor woman, a woman of color, or an abused woman is usually not in a position to defend herself or her parental rights, whether or not she habitually uses drugs. And even if she does use drugs regularly, the present policy is not likely to benefit her or her child, since what she needs is appropriate help and rehabilitation, not punishment.

Yet, that is not what is happening. In New York City, many babies have been taken away from their mothers for insufficient cause and kept in hospitals with insufficient care. Meanwhile, few drug treatment programs accept women and even fewer of them accept pregnant women or women on medicaid. In a study of New York State, Wendy Chavkin (1990) found that of the 78 drug treatment programs on the state's list, 87 percent refused to serve women who were either pregnant, on medicaid, or addicted to crack cocaine. A recent survey of services in Oregon showed that in 1989, 2,140 women were probably using illicit drugs while pregnant; yet, there were only 111 programs with a total of 740 treatment slots for pregnant alcohol or drug users. Even worse, only 21 of these programs had on-site child care facilities and only 134 treatment slots were available for pregnant women with children. The authors of this study estimate that "assuming a 1-year course of therapy, current treatment programs [in Oregon] could accommodate only 13% of the estimated number of recognized [pregnant] users of cocaine, methamphetamine, or heroin" (Slutsker et al., 1993).

The National Association of State Alcohol and Drug Abuse Directors has reported that only about 550,000 of the approximately four million women needing treatment in 1989 received it. Of those four million, 250,000 were pregnant, but only 30,000 received treatment (Bertin, 1993). All this adds up to the fact that there are few resources to enable addicted pregnant women to get off alcohol or drugs, and even fewer for addicted pregnant mothers who need to be caring for their children.

Women often resort to excessive drinking or drug use out of an emotional and physical need sufficient to override the desire to do what is best for their future child. And women's economic status is part of the story at every level. Thus, poor women are more likely to be prosecuted for drug use during pregnancy than affluent women are, although the rates of drug use are comparable (Kolata, 1990). The reason is that reporting of drug or alcohol use is done almost entirely by public hospitals, where poor women go for care, not by private physicians.

How damaging the behavior is also appears to be affected by economic status. A recent study of groups of alcohol-addicted women found that whereas the incidence of fetal alcohol syndrome was 70.9 percent among the children of the lower-class mothers, it was only 4.5 percent among the children of the upper-middle-class mothers (Bingol et al., 1987).

Fetal/Maternal Conflict and Legally Mandated Caesarean Sections

How did embryos and fetuses become separate beings in disregard of the women whose bodies sustain them? And how did pregnant women become criminals against whom the state must protect the fetuses growing within their bodies?

No doubt, the anti-abortion movement has played into this, but there are other factors as well. Until the 1960s, there was no way of knowing anything about an embryo or fetus except by examining the pregnant woman. If you wanted to know whether the fetus moved or its heart beat, you had to ask her, touch her, or put your ear or a stethoscope up against her swollen belly.

Then, in the 1960s, medical scientists developed a first direct test of fetal health when they became able to determine the Rh-antigen status of a fetus. It is important to know the Rh-status of a pregnant woman and her fetus because, if the fetus is Rh-positive, an Rh-negative pregnant woman may develop antibodies against its Rh-antigen that can damage it. Thus, the fetal Rh-test enables physicians to be ready to treat an endangered infant as soon as it is born. Actually, nowadays all pregnant women are given rho-gam, a substance that neutralizes Rh-antibodies, so that the fetus's Rh-status is no longer of special interest, but there is no question that this direct measure of fetal physiology has been important.

Since then, numerous other tests have been developed to assess fetal health directly. But much more important for changing the cultural perception of the fetus than the ability to assess fetal health by means of specific medical tests has been the use of ultrasound imaging. Earlier in the century, obstetricians had used X-rays to visualize fetuses, but that needed to be discontinued when X-rays were shown to increase the incidence of childhood leukemias. (Of course, no one knows for sure that ultrasound is risk-free, but so far no risks have been documented and it has become routine to use ultrasound imaging to visualize fetuses during pregnancy.) Real-life ultrasound imaging has rendered pregnant women transparent and encouraged the culture to bond with "the fetus." Nowadays, fetuses are not only female or male; they swallow, pee, and suck their thumbs, and their pictures can be shown to relatives and friends. (As I said earlier, however, these "pictures" are not pictures in the ordinary sense of the word, but require translation by an expert. See page 56.)

Thus, the anti-abortion movement has not been alone in transforming the cultural status of embryos and fetuses. Routine technological interventions in wanted pregnancies have done this as well, and so has the in vitro fertilization technology. Even more recently, the combination of in vitro fertilization and contractual pregnancy has turned not only eggs and sperm, but also embryos, fetuses, and gestation into commodities that can be ordered from catalogs. An extreme result of this has been a decision, handed down in a case of contested custody by a California judge, in which he stated that a woman who is gestating a fetus derived from another woman's egg is comparable to a baby-sitter. The egg donor, he ruled, is the biological mother.

Setting a pregnant woman and her fetus up as not only separate but as antagonists is of relatively recent origin. As lately as 1979, two adjoining articles were published in the medical journal *Obstetrics & Gynecology*, one by three physicians, the other by an attorney (Lieberman et al., 1979; Shriner, 1979). Both discussed the rare situations in which a physician believes that medical circumstances call for a Caesarean section, but the pregnant or birthing woman refuses to undergo this surgical procedure. And both concluded that, while physicians can use their ingenuity to try to persuade the woman, they cannot open her belly against her will. A Caesarean section performed without the woman's consent would constitute assault and battery.

A mere two years later, an article in the same journal described one of the first legally mandated Caesareans (Bowes and Selegstad, 1981). This situation involved a white woman on welfare who arrived at the University of Colorado Medical Center in labor, without having had prior prenatal care. As the labor progressed, the physician on duty decided a Caesarean was indicated, but the woman was afraid of surgery and refused. A psychiatrist, called in to speak with her, testified that she understood the supposed risk to the baby. Thereupon the hospital obtained an injunction and a hearing was held in the woman's hospital room, presided over by a judge from the Colorado juvenile court, in which the hospital, the woman, and the fetus each were represented by a lawyer. At the conclusion, the judge ruled that a Caesarean was in order, and at that point the woman consented, so that she did not need to be cut open against her will.

Like the prosecutions for "fetal abuse," most court-mandated Caesareans have been performed on poor women, women of color, and foreigners or recent immigrants who speak little or no English. So, again it has been very much a class and race issue.

It is important to recognize that court-mandated interventions in pregnancy and birth are supported not only by "pro-lifers," whose principal concern is for the fetus, but also by some legal experts who support a woman's right to terminate her pregnancy. For example, John A. Robertson (1983), a professor of law at the University of Texas, argues that *Roe v. Wade* guarantees a woman the right to abortion, but that if she "waives" that right by continuing her pregnancy, she is obligated to do whatever is deemed best for the fetus.

There is a problem here, for who is to say what is best? Medical fashions change as do popular beliefs about what is, or is not, good for pregnant women and their fetuses. The amount of weight a woman should gain during pregnancy and how athletic she should be are current examples of this. Of the several pregnant women who have escaped court-mandated Caesareans, either by hiding or because they were lucky enough to go into labor and give birth before the court order could be implemented, all have given birth normally and they and their babies have been fine (Kolder et al., 1987). As physician Helene M. Cole (1990) points out: "Courts are ill-equipped to resolve conflicts concerning obstetrical interventions." Neither physicians nor anyone else can foresee birth outcomes with certainty. So, it is wrong to give medical predictions legal status.

Mandated Caesareans may have been put to rest by a lawsuit instituted by a family with access to the necessary resources (In re: A.C., Appelant, 1990). It involved a woman named Angela Carder who had had cancer during her teens. The cancer went into remission, but years later, after she became pregnant, it was reactivated. When she was 26 weeks pregnant, it became clear that she was not going to survive until the end of her pregnancy. Georgetown Hospital in Washington, D.C., where she was receiving her obstetric care, insisted that she undergo a Caesarean section so as to try to save the fetus. Initially, Carder agreed, but then changed her mind. Despite her refusal and the fact that Carder's parents, her husband, and the medical specialist who was treating her cancer supported her decision, attorneys for the hospital obtained a court order and a staff obstetrician performed the Caesarean. The baby died within two hours of surgery, Carder herself two days later. Her hospital records state that the surgery probably hastened her death. The Federal Appeals Court in the District of Columbia agreed to review the court order under which the surgery took place and in 1990 handed down a very strong opinion against forcing women to undergo Caesarean sections against their will. In addition, the family filed a civil suit and Georgetown Hospital had to pay considerable damages.

This dreadful story may have laid court-mandated Caesareans to rest, but it is easy to extrapolate from court-mandated Caesareans to court-mandated prenatal tests and therapies. This has not happened yet, but it could once a test or therapy becomes standard medical practice. And what if courts one day decide that if no therapy is available and a fetus is predicted to be disabled, the woman must have an abortion

This suggestion is not altogether fanciful. Insurance discrimination against families predicted to have a child with a disability has occurred already. And medical geneticist Paul Billings and his colleagues (1992), in their research into genetic discrimination, have come across an instance that is not very different from this hypothical scenario. In this case, a woman who had borne one child with cystic fibrosis decided to have her fetus tested for this condition during a subsequent pregnancy. When the result indicated that this baby, too, was going to have cystic fibrosis and the woman decided to continue the pregnancy (which, as we have seen, is not unusual for families who have experience caring for a child with cystic fibrosis), the HMO that provided the family's health care announced that it was prepared to pay for an abortion, but not for continued prenatal care or the health care of the future baby because that baby now had what insurers call a pre-existing condition. Only after the family threatened to publicize this decision and, if need be, go to court did the decision get reversed. As prenatal tests proliferate, these kinds of situations are going to become more common, unless we get laws passed to prevent such forms of discrimination and coercion.

Fetal Protection and Workplace Discrimination Against Pregnant Women.

As we have seen, the ability to visualize a fetus and test for certain aspects of its health status makes that fetus more real, more of a person. And when that happens, the pregnant woman seems to become more of a fetal container and less of a person.

Further detrimental effects of this skewed view of pregnancy are illustrated by the so-called fetal protection policies by which women of childbearing age, as a class, have been excluded from certain job categories in which they run the risk of being exposed to radiation, lead, or other toxic chemicals. As we saw earlier, these concerns are not raised because the agents pose dangers to the workers— women and men—but because of the dangers they pose to a "potential" fetus, in case the woman is pregnant. In this construct, all women of childbearing age are deemed potentially pregnant, hence excludable, unless they can show that they have been sterilized. Their life-partner's being sterile is not enough; they must be unable to become pregnant. These concerns are reserved for women employed in jobs, traditionally occupied by men, that pay higher wages and include better benefits than traditional women's jobs do. But attorney Joan E. Bertin (1993) makes the telling point that a woman's employment is often critical to a healthy pregnancy and only she, not her employer, can judge what risks are worth taking to continue in a particular job.

So-called fetal protection policies may have been discouraged by a decision the U.S. Supreme Court rendered in 1991. The court held that it was unlawful for Johnson Controls, Inc., a manufacturer of lead batteries with plants across the country from Vermont to California, to exclude women from working in its lead-battery department (*International Union, UAW v. Johnson Controls*, 1991). Johnson Controls enforced this policy irrespective of the women's marital status or their intentions not to have (more) children, so limiting women's access to more than twenty million jobs (Bertin, 1993).

Meanwhile, scientific and news articles have reported research showing that men's exposure to pesticides, radiation, and toxic workplace chemicals, as well as their consumption of alcohol and drugs, can affect the quality of their sperm and provoke death or disabilities of the fetuses or children they father (Blakeslee,1991).

It stands to reason that sperm is at least as vulnerable to toxic substances and radiation as eggs are, but this society's warped ideology about child-bearing and rearing focuses disproportionately on the procreative functions of women. The usual justifications for what employers refer to as their fetal protection policies are (1) that fetuses may be more vulnerable than adult workers and (2) that all of a woman's eggs are laid down in her ovaries at the time she is born, whereas men produce sperm continually. Therefore, the argument goes, women's eggs age with them and accumulate potential injuries throughout life, whereas sperm is always new.

Both arguments are flawed. Fetuses may be more vulnerable than adults, but no hazards affect exclusively fetuses. The best way to protect fetuses is to clean up workplaces and so protect the workers. As for "aging eggs" and "fresh sperm," men are born with their sperm-precursor cells, just as women are with their eggs. In fact, the sperm-producing cells may be more vulnerable than eggs to radiation or chemical injuries because they keep dividing continuously as they produce the "fresh sperm," and dividing cells are at greater risk from environmental damage than resting cells are.

The Fetus as Patient and Plaintiff?

Many societies control women by controlling procreation, but the medical-legal measures I have been describing are peculiar to the United States. Here, as elsewhere, women not only bear children, but also are principally responsible for their well-being. The inequities intrinsic to capitalism fall most heavily on women and children, and since this country makes few economic, social, and medical provisions for people, it has proportionately more poor women and children than do the other affluent countries, because these offer more adequate social services. In no other industrialized country do so many women give birth without regular, or indeed any, prenatal care. As we saw earlier, this country does not have adequate drug treatment programs for women or men, but especially not for pregnant women. The United States also has a higher proportion of ununionized workers than do other industrialized countries, so that there is less protection for workers' health and safety and for the rights of pregnant workers or workers with children.

The individualistic thinking that prevails in the United States lends itself to blaming women for their low social and economic status and for their own and their children's poor health. This ideology becomes actively punitive when "the fetus" is turned into a patient and plaintiff with its own rights.

To improve this situation will require social measures that deindividualize responsibility. None of the problems I have described can be remedied at the individual level. To solve them requires a commitment at the societal level to care for people who need care and to provide the opportunities people need in order to be able to care for themselves.

Pitting the interests of pregnant women against those of the fetuses they are gestating does not benefit children any more than it does women. Women whom the state considers neglectful of the health of their fetuses, by definition, must be damaging their own health as well. It would be more productive to concentrate on their health needs and to enable them to live healthfully not only while pregnant, but before they become pregnant and after their babies are born as well.

As individuals, we cannot improve women's economic lot; we need to organize for political change. But throughout this work we must insist on women's bodily autonomy. Women must have access to abortions when they do not want to be pregnant, irrespective of their ability to pay. And women must be trusted to make the right decisions, recognizing that they will sometimes err and put their fetuses at risk. Have physicians never put fetuses (or people) at risk, and haven't lawyers or judges?

As far as a fetus's medical and legal rights are concerned, I insist that it does not have any. My criteria simply rely on geography: as long as one cannot get at the fetus without manipulating the woman, she is the only one with the right to make decisions. Once the baby is outside and its well-being no longer impacts on her physical autonomy, then others can begin to speak for it, provided they take responsibility for what they say or do.

A society that forces a woman to bear a child when she does not wish to have one, offers her little or no support when she does, and punishes her when it decides she is acting irresponsibly, is itself guilty of fetal abuse. Unfortunately, nothing in U.S. law mandates equality in access to health resources or care. In fact, the opposite could easily happen when the present, seemingly haphazard and piece-meal, discriminatory practices are regularized and legalized in most of the health reform packages currently being debated in Congress.

Part III

Toward a Political Understanding of Science

Introduction to
Part III

Scientists are not detached, objective observers who stand outside their culture. Our culture shapes our intellectual and practical interests and commitments, and these guide scientific work into specific paths. The pretense of scientific objectivity derives from the fact that, as scientists, we try to separate out the small pieces of nature we look at and specify the ways in which to do that. Anyone else who comes along and repeats what we have done will, indeed, observe similar things as we did. This kind of replicability is taken to mean that our observations, though hopefully original, are in no way idiosyncratic or subjective, since anyone can see what we saw.

What gets omitted from this usual description is that we got to set the terms of the experiment. To do that we made choices and those were affected by economic constraints, cultural commitments, our position and role in the culture, and our personal history.

This is why, as we will see later in this section, women sociobiologists have done different experiments from the ones their male colleagues had been doing and, as a result, have come up with new and different observations and interpretations about animal behavior. Once the women scientists had done this, male observers began to see what they had previously overlooked. This might be taken as confirmation of the objectivity of the new observations: they became possible initially only because the societal and personal experiences of the women scientists were different from those of men, but after that they were part of "objective knowledge."

This assertion leaves out a further essential point. The fact that these women were able to insist on the incompleteness, or even wrongness, of prior observations, to revise them and sometimes turn them upside down, and to have their new interpretations accepted and integrated into the canon was due to the fact that, by the time these women scientists came along, the women's movement had made major inroads into the culture, so that their male colleagues had to reckon with them and listen to their scientific pronouncements. When the psychologist Ruth Herschberger made similar points in her book *Adam's Rib*, published in 1948, she was ignored as were the feminists who had tried to counter Darwin in the nineteenth century.

In the essays in this section, I try to give specific examples of the interplay of science and technology with other cultural and political commitments. "Of Genies and Bottles" was first published in a collection dedicated to the memory of Margaret Lowe Benston, a Canadian physical chemist, computer scientist, women's studies scholar, and community activist. Benston was profoundly interested in the mutual interplay between politics and science/technology and did whatever she could to further women's participation in both.

The next two essays describe the alchemy by which cultural meanings assigned to signifiers such as sex and race are translated into the biology of "difference." This process is also reflected in my review of Donna Haraway's *Primate Visions*. As published here, this essay represents my original review. The version that appeared in the *Village Voice* was somewhat different.

The last two essays were written more specifically to further the integration of the new feminist scholarship in the natural sciences with that in other disciplines, and to help redefine what counts as knowledge and gets taught to students as significant and important. In them, I try to give practical suggestions for how to improve communication between natural scientists and "the public," which includes educators in the social sciences and humanities.

I have stressed before, and repeat here, that it is essential that more people than those who are now part of the decision-making process participate in deciding what science gets done, and whether and how it should be implemented in technology. Scientific work and its technological consequences have too great an impact on everyone to leave these portentous decisions to scientists and their financial partners in government and private industry.

Thus, this entire final section, though diverse in its subject matter, focuses on the cultural and political construction and meaning of science/technology and on the dynamic interplay of scientific work with scientific and political ideology and practice.

Of Genies and Bottles

Technology, Values and Choices

We need to escape from the techno-fatalism embodied in the common sentiment that "the genie is out of the bottle and we cannot put it back." We cannot afford to accept the notion that a technology, once initiated, will grind on; that its course cannot be changed and that it certainly cannot be stopped.

This is especially necessary with reference to biotechnology, which will intrude increasingly into our daily lives as scientists and entrepreneurs (who are often one and the same) develop it further. But in order to affect the course of this, or any, technology, we need to keep informed, so that we can say "no" whenever and wherever we want to, and do not become overwhelmed by the quantity of specialized knowledge involved. And when we oppose specific scientific ventures or technologies, we must recognize that we are motivated by responsible citizenship, not by a technological nihilism that has come to be misnamed Luddism.

Rehabilitating the Luddites

Before going on to draw some specific examples from biotechnology, I want to digress briefly and try to redeem the reputation of Luddism. Those of us who oppose certain technologies are often called Luddites, but the time has come to stop defending ourselves against that charge and own Luddism as a proud heritage worth perpetuating.

Luddism was a social movement in the early nineteenth century, at the beginning of the industrial revolution in England. The Luddists were artisans in the English Midlands, in Lancashire, Nottinghamshire, and Yorkshire. They are usually described as lawless men who broke machines, especially the weaving frames and stocking frames. However, these frames were being brought into the new factories to replace the tools these artisans had been using in their workshops, which often were part of their homes. Luddism was a political movement that was grounded in a rebellion against the introduction of the factory system. The Luddites opposed the hiring of wage laborers to replace skilled artisans working in their own shops.

As the British historian E.P. Thompson writes, the new cottonmills "were centres of exploitation, monstrous prisons in which children were confined.... [They] reduced the industrious artisan to 'a dependent state.' A way of life was at stake, and... opposition to particular machines...[was] very much more than a particular group of skilled workers defending their own livelihood. These machines symbolised the encroachment of the factory system."[1] Thompson tells us, for example, that one Luddite in 1800 sold "a prospering business rather than employ machinery which he regarded as 'a means of oppression on the part of the rich and of corresponding degradation and misery to the poor.'" This was not just "a blind opposition to machinery," but an organized opposition to "the 'freedom' of the capitalist to destroy the customs of the trade, whether by new machinery, by the factory system, or by unrestricted competition, beating down wages, undercutting his rivals, and undermining standards of craftmanship."[2]

The Luddites were opposing the factory owners for degrading skills and for replacing skilled craftsmen with young boys and other unskilled workers. They demanded a minimum wage, control of sweatshops that employed women and children, a ten-hour workday, arbitration of grievances, efforts to find work for skilled craftsmen, prohibition of shoddy work, and the right to organize into trade unions. For this reason, in their so-called riots, the Luddites targeted the weaving frames of manufacturers who had lowered their wages, not of those who hadn't. And even within a single shop, they sometimes broke only frames of a master who had hired low-paid workers, not those belonging to masters who hadn't. So, we need to recognize in Luddism an important historical example of a selective opposition to technologies that people decided were constricting their lives rather than freeing them.

Like the Luddites of old, most of us who oppose some of today's technological "advances" are not opposed to technology per se. We simply insist on exercising our right, if not our civic obligation, to discriminate among technologies. And we must remember that, though the Luddites failed to stop the factory system, some of the regulations and improvements for which they agitated were put in place.

The Question of "Choice"

That raises the question, on what basis we want to discriminate among technologies and—more important—who that "we" is who can do the discriminating. When we think about what values should frame our opposition, we need to come to terms with the standard questions: Isn't all knowledge good? Shouldn't we encourage scientists to learn and find out all they can and decide later what knowledge to implement in practice and turn into technology?

That might be nice, but unfortunately it isn't how the world works. Particularly in a profit-oriented economy—and at present that's what exists just about everywhere—any knowledge from which scientists and entrepreneurs can envisage generating a profit is likely to be exploited.

Some people argue that, if a technology can be made to generate a profit, by definition that means that people want it. But that is naive. With present means of advertising and marketing, it is not difficult to make enough people "want" whatever entrepreneurs wish to sell. And that's as true of the new biotechnologies such as in vitro fertilization, embryo selection, and genetic screening as it is of cigarettes, which we all know are bad for people.

So, those of us who want people to be able to discriminate not only among technologies, but to go further and decide what knowledge is worth knowing, have an enormous task ahead of us. We need to raise people's awareness of the issues at stake as well as to give people access to the facts and to information that will enable them to make reasoned choices so that they are not forced always to choose the most widely advertised alternative.

To make this concrete, let us look at just one family of technologies that is growing by leaps and bounds: predictive genetic tests. Let me repeat from my previous discussion, these tests are not meant to diagnose an illness or disability, but to *predict* the likelihood that it will occur. Such predictions are usually made by means of prenatal tests or by testing healthy people who are thought to have a greater than usual likelihood of developing some condition in the future.

The benefits of such predictive tests are problematic, because usually the predictions can only assign probabilities that a given condition may occur, but do not indicate whether it will in fact occur or how disabling it will be if it does. The tests can offer statistical information, but this is a questionable benefit to the individuals who are being tested.

On the other hand, these kinds of predictions open the door to genetic discrimination—discrimination against people because of a perceived risk that they will develop a genetically-linked health problem some time in the future. Though the tests are relatively new and only a few of them are at present available, there already are documented instances of otherwise qualified people being denied employment, health or life insurance, the right to adopt a child, or even a driver's license on the basis of a predictive genetic test.[3]

Let us think for a moment about the meaning of the concept of choice once a technology or medical practice has become accepted as the "right" way to do things. How about the choice to refuse predictive tests? How real, at present, is the "choice" of a middle-class woman over 35 *not* to have amniocentesis? What about the choice of a woman over 50 *not* to have a mammogram? How about a pregnant woman's choice to go into a bar and order a drink— not to get drunk, just to have a drink, or maybe even two drinks? I am purposely picking examples where there are still arguments on both sides, but where we hear the arguments on one side much more loudly and more often than those on the other.

These are all so-called life-style choices, though they really go much deeper than that. But what about a woman's choice to continue or *discontinue* in a job that may pose health hazards to a developing fetus, if she needs the income and no safer and equally well-paid job is available? Are any of these really questions of choice? Choice is a catchword in our liberal, individualistic society, but it is rarely a practical reality in many matters that have a profound impact on our lives.

Choices need to be made at the beginning, before a technology becomes so entrenched that cultural norms call for only one approved way to choose. They need to be social choices, not individual choices. And we need democratic mechanisms for making these choices as a society. The individual person's right to choose, precious as it is, is not enough.

How to Put Genies Back into their Bottles

Lest we become discouraged, let us look at a situation where the level of technology has been reduced—at a genie that has been shoved a little way back into the bottle. I refer to the demedicalization of childbirth. It is now possible to give birth in less technological and medicalized ways than I was able to do some thirty-five years ago. Of course, it is also possible to have a much *more* technological and medicalized birth than I did. In many teaching hospitals, the Caesarean rate has tripled or quadrupled since those days, and even women who do not have a Caesarean section can be exposed to technological interventions all along the way. But the women's health movement did open the possibility of reducing the level of technology, so that now a woman can consult a midwife instead of an obstetrician, and birth her baby at home with little by way of technology. And she can do this not just because she is too poor to pay for a medicalized pregnancy and birth, which is the way it used to be thirty years ago, but in an informed way and by choice. And though this choice is not available to every woman, and not every woman would wish to make it, the women's health movement has made a big difference by supporting women who want to avoid routine technological interventions in their pregnancies and births.

What to Do?

This example shows that to gain control or make changes we need to organize and work politically. For that, hospital or laboratory ethics or bioethics committees are not enough. We need advocacy and education at the grass roots, or as close to them as possible, so that ordinary people do not look on technology as their salvation or enemy, and in either case as an aspect of fate.

When it comes to biotechnology, one of the large questions we need to address is this: Should we be working on high-tech solutions to any health problems, while death over much of the globe, and right here in the United States, is often due to preventable causes—hunger, malnutrition, poverty, contaminated food and water, and so forth?

So long as the scientific entrepreneurs continue to develop and implement extravagantly expensive technologies, these will be of use only to people who can afford to pay for them. We must do all we can to oppose so-called solutions to health problems that are so expensive that they, by definition, ration health care.

We keep hearing that socialism doesn't work. But capitalism surely doesn't work, when companies can make profits by marketing expensive, and sometimes health-damaging, technologies that skew our needs and priorities.

We need a lot of activism and a revitalized "Science for the People" movement that produces science shops and science fairs whose message is not just "Ain't Science Great?" but that give people the information they need to make critical decisions about how they want to see our common resources used. And, of course, this information must be presented in an intelligible and relevant form.

There is a problem here, and that is that it is difficult to convince people they should know, and indeed would enjoy knowing, about the birds and the bees and the flowers when these people live in environments where they never see a bird or a bee or a flower. It is a real question how to arouse an appreciation of the fascinating and elegant ways nature functions, and to stimulate a desire to control science and technology, in people to whom nature is utterly abstract while science and technology, though alien and overpowering, are part of the daily environment. And another thing: it is hard to know how to make people understand the need to make choices about whether to devise and implement technologies, when technology is much more real and "God-given" to them than are the natural functions for which technologies are meant to substitute or on which technology is meant to expand.

These are crucial problems that don't get talked about enough. Perhaps the first genie that needs to be put back into its bottle is our alienation from the ways nature and our bodies function. Presumably technologies get developed to improve on what exists in nature. But if people have no idea what that is or was, how can they decide whether the technologies are improvements? So, "choice" may be a key word in our society, but people can only make choices when they know the alternatives among which to choose.

Activists for social justice need to look critically at who stands to gain, and who stands to lose, from each specific technical innovation, and to spread that information. We must help people to question the decisions to develop specific technologies and support them when they decide to oppose these decisions. By doing that, we do not become irresponsible nay-sayers and "Luddites," opposed to all forms of technology. We become responsible teachers and advocates for fairness and justice.

Gender Ideology and the Biology of Sex Differences

In this essay I want to focus on three aspects of science. I will begin with a theoretical discussion about how we make science, because science is not just out there; it is a human, cultural enterprise. Then I want to look at the fact that only specific sorts of concepts of nature lend themselves to making science and only certain aspects of nature get included in science. I will illustrate this by discussing how gender ideology shapes our understanding of the biology of sex differences all the way from the level of populations and whole organisms, that is, evolution and sociobiology, to the molecular level—chromosomes, genes, and DNA. Finally, I'll sum up and say a few words about where that leaves us when we try to think about what science can tell us and about how to use that knowledge responsibly.

* * *

Western science, which is what most people nowadays mean when they use the word "science," is the effort to understand nature in order to harness that knowledge for use.

The distinction between science and technology, which is so dear to the hearts of many present-day scientists, was invented in the nineteenth century for a variety of historical reasons that I won't discuss here. But the fact is that from Francis Bacon until now the purpose of Western science has been to gain power over nature in order to use it.

However, science is not a haphazard set of observations that people then put to use. It is an effort to construct a picture, or model, that can provide a logical and coherent system of explanations of natural phenomena. To construct such a model, or metaphor, scientists cannot just hold up a mirror to nature. Rather, we sift nature through something like a coarse sieve, perhaps a colander. Everything we fail to notice or analyze falls through and we then construct our picture of nature by formulating coherent stories out of what stays behind.

Of course, our stories have to correspond in important ways to what has gone before—to what we know already—and also to other people's experiences and stories. So, science, in the main, is about shared experiences of nature.

But our understanding of nature is, by its nature, even more limited. We construct not only our interpretations, but also the very nature we choose to interpret. Working scientists don't just "look at nature." We first circumscribe and define what aspects of it we will examine. That is true even if we work "in the field," studying ecology or animal behavior. If we work in laboratories or do theoretical calculations at our desks, we further select, or indeed deliberately create the models, the metaphors, which we allow to stand in for nature as we do our scientific work.

Now, the very idea that one can form a coherent and comprehensible picture of nature rests on assumptions which not all cultures share. The British biologist and historian of science Joseph Needham suggested many years ago that probably one reason that what we call science arose in the West, despite the fact that at that time the Chinese had a much keener sense of how nature works, as exemplified by their technology, is the assumption, fundamental to Western science, that nature obeys regularities.[1]

Regularities are what makes it possible for scientists to formulate the so-called Laws of Nature, laws that are quite analogous to the laws by which human societies operate. Our Laws of Nature "permit" certain kinds of events to take place and "forbid" others. We say that falling bodies "obey" the laws of gravity and if a body rises up in the air, we look for what made it do that, convinced that in a lawful universe it couldn't have done it on its own.

Needham points out that, as late as 1730, a Swiss court prosecuted a rooster for laying an egg (and convicted him and burned him at the stake), which suggests that the legal metaphor at one time was taken quite literally. He assumes, and I agree, that the reason the Laws of Nature come easily to the Western mind is based on our cultural belief in a human-like being, who created the world and set it moving along a lawful course, so that it is at least in principle comprehensible and predictable by humans made in His image.

Although most of us, and surely most scientists, no longer believe this literally, it underlies our implicit assumptions and thinking.

* * *

I want to give you a few examples of the way gender ideology—which is an integral part of our belief system—informs the ways in which biologists and chemists describe differences, and not just between female and male organisms. This ideology also permeates our understanding about the organs, cells, and even the molecules that are implicated in "sex difference"—so between ovaries and testes, eggs and sperm, the so-called sex hormones, and the sex chromosomes and genes, that is, DNA molecules.

But while I review these ideologically laden concepts, I want you to bear in mind that such sexist descriptions of what these scientists would call nature are not being put forward by foolish people or by bigots. Individual scientists may be that, but the more significant point is that these descriptions and analyses are being offered by ordinary scientists, men and women who—because they have been taught that science is by its nature objective—have been trained not to look for the ways in which societal realities and beliefs affect the ways scientists see nature and interpret it.

Let us start with Darwin's theory of evolution by natural selection—in other words, the theory that describes the changes organisms have experienced over time. Darwin's theory operates with three principles:

1. Random variations occur among organisms within a species and those variations are inherited from one generation to the next.

2. Organisms live in an economy of scarcity, which means that they must compete. This leads to

the so-called struggle for existence. This formulation relies heavily on theories put forth by the Reverend Thomas Malthus in his *Essay on the Principles of Population*, first published in 1798, and by Adam Smith, two social theorists of the time.

3. This competition and struggle is the weeding out process that leads to "the survival of the fittest" (a phrase coined by yet another social theorist, Herbert Spenser). It is important to understand that in Darwinian terms superior "fitness" is assigned to those among the variants who survive to have off-spring, who themselves survive long enough to have off-spring and so pass on the traits that have been selected in the struggle.

Obviously, there is a lot of ideology in this. There is the assumption that nature operates in a context of scarcity and competition, and that organisms survive through struggle. And since Darwin's day many philosophers and historians have commented on this, among the first being Marx and Engels, but later also Bertrand Russell and others.

We get to gender ideology in the second part of Darwin's *Origin of Species*, which is where he introduces the concept of what he calls "sexual selection." The point is that sexual reproduction—two organisms coming together to create a third, different from either parent—is at the center of Darwin's theory of evolution because who mates with whom, and how those choices are made, is crucial to the path evolution will take.

And this is where Darwin puts forth the Victorian paradigm of the ever passionate, sexually indiscriminate male, who is always in active competition with all other males in his pursuit of any and all available females, while females are by their nature coy, passive, and unenthusiastic about sex, but choosy in that they go for the winner.

This basic difference between females and males automatically leads to more active competition among males than among females, since the males compete not only for resources, but also for females (who thereby become just another resource). For this reason males are the vanguard that guides the evolution of the species, while females get pulled along by mating with the most successful males.

This nineteenth-century picture has been modified somewhat in the contemporary avatar of Darwinian thinking, sociobiology.[2] We still have active, competitive males and coy, passive females, but the rationale, though still based in economics, has changed somewhat.

We are no longer with Adam Smith and the free market, but have moved on to investment and banking economics. Now the reason for the difference between females and males is that females are said to be a "scarce resource," and not because there are fewer females than males—there usually aren't—but because females in their lifetime produce fewer eggs than males can produce sperm. And not only that, but females also "invest" more in each of our large, yolky eggs than males do in each of their lean, sprightly sperm.

So, males have evolved to be promiscuous because their optimum strategy is to diversify their investments by mating with as many females as they can and so fertilizing as many eggs as possible.

Females, on the other hand, have evolved to be coy and discriminating as they try to catch their man and make him help them guard the few precious investments—that is to say, offspring—each female can procure in her lifetime. So, females are by nature faithful homebodies, while males are by nature promiscuous swingers.

More recently, this contemporary version has been challenged by Sarah Blaffer Hrdy and a number of other feminist sociobiologists.[3] Having observed animals in their natural environments rather than in laboratories or zoos, they point out that female animals are not passive, coy, and compliant. Females, they argue, also compete, initiate and terminate sexual contacts, solicit males, are promiscuous, and so on. So, these feminist sociobiologists have tried to get rid of the sexist metaphors, though they pretty much stick with the economic metaphors.

* * *

Let us now leave the level of organisms, where observer bias is hard to avoid, and move on to the more "objective" realms of organs, cells, and molecules. And let us start by looking at descriptions of embryonic development.

Here we have a standard story you find in the textbooks. According to this story, vertebrate embryos (and we will confine ourselves to them) start out sexually ambiguous and bipotential. There is no way you can tell whether they are going to be male or female just by looking at them.

Then in humans, during the seventh week of embryonic development, says the story, in males, under the influence of the Y chromosome, something happens so that part of the undifferentiated gonad develops into a testis and the rest of the fetal gonad atrophies. This fetal testis soon begins to secrete so-called androgens or male sex hormones, and these masculinize one set of embryonic ducts so that they develop into sperm ducts and male external genitalia, that is, the scrotal sac and penis. In some more modern versions of this story, these fetal androgens also somehow affect certain parts of the brain and "masculinize" them.

The standard story goes on to say that if, at this critical point at seven weeks, nothing happens, then a while later another part of the undifferentiated gonad differentiates into ovaries. And without the hormonal influence of the embryonic testis, another set of embryonic ducts differentiates into fallopian tubes, a uterus, vagina and the external female genitalia, that is labia, and a clitoris.

You will find this story also in textbooks written by women, some of them feminists. So what's wrong?

First, the nomenclature of the so-called sex hormones is peculiar. As the biologist Anne Fausto-Sterling has pointed out, we have "androgen"—the generator of males, but there is no gynogen—no generator of females. Instead, the chemical and physiological counterpart of androgen, the so-called female hormone, is called estrogen, from estrus, the Greek word for frenzy or gadfly.[4]

There is another point about the naming of the so-called sex hormones.[5] These were discovered late in the nineteenth century, when scientists found that extracting testes and ovaries with fat solvents yielded different substances. These findings encouraged the hope that the differences in these substances would explain the differences between males and females. But other scientists soon discovered that males and females have both substances, only in somewhat different, but overlapping, proportions. Further, these hormones are closely related to each other chemically, are synthesized in the adrenals and the liver as well as the gonads, and are interconvertible. In the late 1920s, it was discovered that the richest source from which to isolate the so-called female hormone estrogen is stallions' urine. That destroyed the hope that sex hormones could account for the difference between the sexes.

Another problem with the standard story is that, in mammals, the developing embryo is bathed in maternal hormones, both estrogen and progesterone. Male embryos must overcome this influence, but female embryos surely do not develop in a hormonal vacuum, as the standard story implies.

It is worth noting that the maculinist story I have just laid out has its feminist counterpart, put forward in the late 1960s by Mary Jane Sherfey, a physician and feminist. She uses this same developmental story to argue that the basic developmental pattern is female and that males are a variant on it, brought on by the Y chromosome and fetal androgens.

I would argue that neither of these stories describes the situation. All embryonic development is active and occurs by way of processes that involve many reactions, influences, and decision points. Nothing "just happens." And neither pattern is more "basic" than the other.

* * *

Let us now move on and look at the production of the two kinds of gametes—sperm and eggs—and at their union during fertilization.

Of course, here we start with the minute, nimble, active sperm and the large, sessile, yolky egg. Ejaculation "launches" sperm on its dauntless voyage up the female reproductive tract, while eggs are "released" or "shed" from the ovary and sit around in the fallopian tube, waiting for sperm to come along. And if no sperm arrives, the egg goes to pieces. If sperm arrives in time, then the egg continues to sit there, while a sperm bores its way in, madly flailing its tail. What is more, sperm is being produced all the time, whereas females are born with all their eggs laid down in their ovaries. So, sperm is always fresh, while eggs get older every day.[6]

What's wrong? Again, lots of things. For one thing, sperm isn't all that active and eggs don't just sit there. Both must move and their movement and ability to get together depend on the active participation of the entire female reproductive tract—cervix, uterus, fallopian tubes—with its secretions and motions. This is why pelvic inflammatory disease and the inflammation due to gonorrhea so often lead to infertility. Fertilization itself also is an active process that requires the participation of both egg and sperm. Their cell membranes send out microtubules, the two cells fuse, their nuclei first change position and then meld—a lot has to happen.

Incidentally, lest you think I am making these stories up a paper published in a scientific journal in 1987 had the title "The Existential Decision of a Sperm." Its authors discuss how sperm "decides" to fertilize an egg. Note, also, that English grammar requires us to say that sperm "fertilizes" (active), whereas eggs "are fertilized" (passive).

Another point is that the standard story emphasizes the equivalence of the contributions of sperm and egg to the next generation. This emphasis is achieved by focusing on the nuclei and ignoring the fact that the egg, in addition to its nucleus, contributes its entire cytoplasm, including another set of genetic particles with their own complement of DNA; there is no equivalent male contribution. The egg cytoplasm and its subcellular structures affect the first cell divisions of the early embryo and nourish the embryo until it differentiates sufficiently to establish contact with the stored yolk or, in mammals, with the nutrients the mother supplies via the placenta.

As for the story about old eggs and fresh sperm, that is nonsense. Although sperm is generated continuously, it is generated from cells, called spermatogonia, that are laid down in the embryo and that age just like the primordial ova do. Indeed, although this fresh sperm/old eggs argument has been used to justify the exclusion of women from workplaces that have traditionally been open only to men on the grounds that the work might damage their aging eggs, as I said in Part II, the story is probably the other way around. Since the sperm-generating cells are undergoing active cell division much of the time, they are probably *more* prone to injury by environmental mutagens than the eggs are.

So, for the production of eggs and sperm, as for their fusion during fertilization, the standard story describes our society more than it does the biological events.

* * *

Finally, let us move on to the surely more objective realm of molecules—that is, to chromosomes and DNA.

Here we meet an article published in the scientific journal *Cell* in December 1987, by David Page and his co-workers—men and women—at MIT.[7] They claim to describe what they call a "sex switch," located on the Y chromosome (the chromosome that is present only in males and is therefore assumed to "determine" maleness). This article was picked up immediately in the scientific weekly *Science*, as well as in the *New York Times*, *Boston Globe*, and other newspapers.

In the article the scientists claim that this gene, located on the Y chromosome, decides not maleness but sex. Their story says that the indifferent embryonic gonad, under the influence of this specific gene on the Y chromosome, "determines" the development of testes. If this gene is absent, the embryo develops ovaries. The X chromosome doesn't do anything, or perhaps it inhibits the gene on the Y chromosome.

There is a fundamental problem with this scenario because it ignores the presence of X chromosomes in both males and females. It also posits that people who have two X chromosomes, whom we call females, are equivalent to people who have only one X chromosome and neither a Y nor a second X chromosome. However, such people have what is called Turner syndrome. They are female by the definition that they have a uterus and external female genitalia, but as adults they have neither ovaries nor

174

testes, and therefore no reproductive cells (eggs or sperm). In other words, the second X chromosome in females must do *something*. But in this article, the Y chromosome is referred to as a "binary switch" which by its presence or absence "controls" sex. Rather, it would seem that the Y chromosome starts differentiation along one kind of path, while the second X is instrumental in starting it along another.

Two years later, two other groups of scientists showed that the region on the Y chromosome, the "gene" of Page and his co-workers, is not the "sex switch," because some people who lack this region still develop as males.[8] But that simply meant that they went looking for it elsewhere on the Y chromosome.

In August of 1994, scientists finally have come up with a "gene for femaleness," located on the X chromosome, that not only "determines" femaleness, but that is even capable of overriding the erstwhile "sex switch" on the Y chromosome.[9] Of course, in both cases, it is absurd to imagine that unique genes "determine" a process as complex as sex differentiation.

* * *

Before concluding, let us look briefly at the way scientists have dealt with reproduction, and what they therefore call sex, in plants and bacteria. Obviously, here there are no penises and vaginas or eggs and sperm. But once again, the same active/ passive dichotomy becomes the criterion.

In plants, the question revolves around pollination. Plants (or parts of plants) that produce pollen are called male; plants (or parts of plants) that "are pollinated," female. But what about bacteria, which usually reproduce quite literally by dividing into two? Occasionally bacteria do something different: two of them will come together and exchange DNA, or rather, one of them grows a small projection called a pilus, through which it transfers some of its DNA into the other. I leave it to you to guess which is called male.

* * *

So where does this leave us? Is science a useless exercise that can only reproduce social ideology, while offering us its metaphors for nature, whereas nature, as we conceptualize it, is only a metaphor for social reality?

This question is being actively debated in the new social studies of science. One school, operating by analogy with post-modern literary criticism, looks upon nature purely as text, and science purely as stories. For it, there are no more or less accurate descriptions, no better or worse science. Everything is stories.

In this view, the kind of social analysis I have been doing and the awareness it can generate simply change the contours of the narrative field that determine what stories become permissible. Now feminist sociobiologists can see, and tell us, that female monkeys are competitive and promiscuous and initiate sexual contacts. Now molecular geneticists can look for sex-determining genes on X as well as Y chromosomes. But they will produce only *different* stories, not better or more correct ones.

Having been trained as a biologist, I cannot go that far. Nature exists. And there *are* better and worse, more and less accurate, interpretations of it. Perhaps the best way to judge them is by their effects as we implement them in technology and draw other practical consequences from them.

Judged by those standards, we have been doing badly indeed. Scientists have focused narrowly. Our science has produced lots of gadgets, but we have ignored wider contexts and interrelationships. And so we find ourselves in the midst of multiple ecological and other crises, because we are constantly trying to separate what physicians conveniently call the "effects," by which they mean the benefits of a treatment, from its "side effects," the unanticipated results or those we would gladly do without.

But in the larger picture, *there are no side effects*, just as *there are no waste products*. All effects are equally there, all products need to be reckoned with. We cannot afford to acknowledge only the ones we like and look away from the ones we don't. So, my point is not that all stories are equally good and equally true, but that, in comparing and evaluating them, it will not do to look only at the parts we like and ignore the others.

That means that we have to insist that critical evaluations of science and technology must be integrated into the process of making science. And these evaluations should not just be made by scientists, as scientists tend to argue they should, but by everyone who must live with the consequences of the knowledge scientists produce and with its implementation in technology.

How could we get a better handle on what nature is like? One serious problem is the narrow slice of humanity that is now able to become people whose descriptions of nature we believe—predominantly male, upper-middle-class Euro-Americans, educated in institutions that validate one specific tradition of education and knowledge. We need to expand the sources of observation, so that more *different* kinds of people can tell us what they see out there.

Other descriptions of nature exist as well as other technologies. There is women's knowledge about nature that we acquire in our garden plots, our kitchens and sickrooms; farmers' knowledge about nature; indigenous knowledge about nature that exists to some extent even in Europe, but surely in the Americas, Asia, Africa, and Australia—indeed, wherever people have lived for a long time and have tried to understand the weather, plants, animals, human diseases, and so on.

We often call their knowledge superstition and ours science. And as I said before, I am not saying that all sources of knowledge are equally valid, all descriptions of nature equally true. But we need to become a good deal more critical about the sources of our knowledge about nature and a great deal more open to descriptions offered by people whose ideological backgrounds and real-life experiences are different from ours.

To be both useful and benign, science needs to draw on the experiences of people who are usually disqualified from making science, like women, or farmers, or workers of both sexes.

Constructs
of Race Difference

Since its beginnings, the science of genetics has been caught up in the dialectic between likeness and difference. When people think about heredity, what they hope scientists will explain is how it is that Johnny has grandpa's nose and aunt Mary's chin. But they also want to understand how come little Susie doesn't look like anyone else in the family.

And scientists have put a good deal of effort into examining the biological basis of various characteristics that have cultural and political significance, including differences between so-called races, as well as between women and men. In doing so, they have often made it appear as though differences in power between individuals or groups of people were the inevitable and natural results of biological difference, and hence of genes.

This became critically important in the eighteenth century, when support for the aims of the revolutions fought for liberty, equality, fraternity, and for the Rights of Man needed to be reconciled with the obvious inequalities between nations, races, and the sexes. It is well to realize that as late as the sixteenth century, authors described the peoples of Africa as superior in wit and intelligence to the inhabitants of northern climes, arguing that the hot, dry climate "enlivened their temperament,"[1] and two centuries later Rousseau still rhapsodized about the Noble Savage. The industrialization of Europe and North America depended on the exploitation of

179

the native populations of the Americas and Africa. So it became imperative to draw distinctions between that small number of men who were created equal and everyone else. By the nineteenth century, the Noble Savage was a lying, thieving Indian, and Africans and enslaved African Americans were ugly, slow, stupid, and in every way inferior to Europeans or Euro-Americans. Distinctions also needed to be drawn between women and men, since irrespective of class and race, women were not included among "all men" who were created equal.

In the preceding essay, I focused on biological constructs of sex difference. Let us now look at race and begin by considering the so-called Races of Man. The writer Allan Chase dates scientific racism from the publication of Malthus's *Essay on Population* in 1798 and argues that it focused on class distinctions among Europeans rather than on distinctions between Europeans and their decendants and the peoples native to Africa, America, and Asia.[2] On the other hand, Stephen Jay Gould attributes the first scientific ranking of races to Linnaeus some forty years earlier.[3] Linnaeus went further and arranged the races into different sub-species. He also wrote that Africans, whom he called *Homo sapiens afer*, are "ruled by caprice," whereas Europeans (*Homo sapiens europaeus*) are "ruled by customs," and that African men are indolent and African women are shameless and lactate profusely.

Both Linnaeus and Malthus did their work more than two centuries after the beginning of the European slave trade, which became an important part of the economies of Europe and the Americas. But their work was contemporary with the intellectual and civic ferment that led to the American and French revolutions of 1776 and 1789 and to the revolution that overthrew slavocracy in Haiti in 1791. As the Guyanan political thinker and activist Walter Rodney pointed out, it is wrong to think "that Europeans enslaved Africans for racist reasons." They did so for economic reasons, since without a supply of free African labor, they would not have been able "to open up the New World and to use it as a constant generator of wealth.... Then, having become utterly dependent on African labour, Europeans at home and abroad found it necessary to rationalize that exploitation in racist terms."[4]

Physicians and biologists helped to legitimate such rationalizations by constructing criteria, such as skull volume, brain size, and many others, by which they tried to prove scientifically that Africans are inferior to Europeans. Gould's *Mismeasure of Man* describes some of these measurements and documents their often patently racist intent. Gould also illustrates the ways in which, for example, the distinguished nineteenth-century French anatomist Paul Broca discarded criteria by which white men could not be made to rank highest. And he shows how Broca and the American craniometer Samuel George Morton fudged and fiddled with their data in order to make the rankings come out as these men knew they must: Euro-American men on top, next native American men, and then African-American men. Women presented a problem: though clearly Euro-American women ranked below Euro-American men, were they to be above or below men of the other races? A colleague of Broca's addressed this conundrum in 1881. "Men of the black races," he wrote, "have a brain scarcely heavier than that of white women."[5]

In 1854, Dr. Samuel Cartwright, an American physician, wrote an article entitled "Diseases and Peculiarities of the Negro," in which he asserted that a defect in the "atmospherization of the blood conjoined with a deficiency of cerebral matter in the cranium...led to that debasement of mind which has rendered the people of Africa unable to take care of themselves."[6] And racialist biology did not end with slavery. Writing during World War II, the Swedish economist Gunnar Myrdal marveled that the American Red Cross did not accept African Americans as blood donors. "After protests," he wrote, "it now accepts Negro blood but segregates it to be used exclusively for Negro soldiers. This is true at a time when the United States is at war, and the Red Cross has a semi-official status."[7] The American Red Cross continued to separate the blood of African and European Americans until December 1950, when the binary classification into "Negro" and "white" was deleted from the donor forms. Howard Zinn has pointed out the irony that, in fact, an African-American physician, Charles Drew, developed the blood banking system in the first place.[8]

What can we say now about the biology of race differences? Looking at all the evidence, there are none.[9] Demographers, politicians, and social scientists may want to continue using "race" to sort people, but as a biological concept it has no meaning. Human beings (*Homo sapiens*) are genetically a relatively homogeneous species. If Europeans were to disappear overnight, the genetic composition of the species would hardly change. About 75 percent of known genes are the same in all humans. The remaining 25 percent are known to exist in more than one form, but all the forms can be found in all groups, though sometimes in different proportions.[10] Another way to say this is that, because of the extent of interbreeding that has happened among human populations over time, our genetic diversity is pretty evenly distributed over the entire species. An occasional, relatively recent mutation may still be somewhat localized within a geographic area, but about 90 percent of the variations known to occur among humans as a whole occur also among the individuals of any one national or racial group.[11]

Another important point is that for any scientific measurement of race differences, we first have to construct what we mean by race. Does the least trace of African origins make someone black, or does the least trace of European origins make someone white? The former definition is more widely accepted in the United States, but it is a social convention and not a fact of biology.

The U.S. census for 1870 contained a third category, "Mulatto," for "all persons having any perceptible trace of African blood" and warned that "important scientific results depend on the correct determination of this class."[12] The U.S. census for 1890 collected information separately for "quadroons and octaroons"—people one in four of whose grandparents or one in eight of whose great-grandparents were African, "while in 1930, any mixture of white and some other race was to be reported according to the race of the parent who was not white."[13] Finally, in 1970 the Statistical Policy Division of the Office of Management and the Budget warned that racial "classifications should not be interpreted as being scientific or anthropological in nature."[14]

How, then, should we interpret such statistics as that "black men under age 45 are ten times more likely to die from the effects of high blood pressure than white men," that "black women suffer twice as many heart attacks as white women," and that "a variety of common cancers are more frequent among blacks...than whites,"[15] especially when some scientists and the media keep stressing the genetic origin of these conditions? Does not that prove that there are inherent, biological differences between blacks and whites, as groups?

The fact is, it doesn't. It is unfortunate and misleading that U.S. health statistics usually are presented in terms of the quasi-biological triad of age, race, and sex, without providing data about employment, income, housing, and the other prerequisites for healthful living. Even though there are genetic components to skin color, as there are to eye or hair color, there is no biological reason to assume that any one of these is more closely related to health status than any other. Skin color ("race") is no more likely to be biologically related to the tendency to develop high blood pressure than eye color is.

To come up with rational explanations, we need to take account of the fact that the median income of African Americans since 1940 has been less than two-thirds that of Americans of European descent. Disproportionate numbers of African Americans live in more polluted and run-down neighborhoods, work in more polluted and stressful work places, and have fewer escape routes out of these living and work situations than Euro-Americans have. Furthermore, African Americans at all levels of society experience stress arising from their history and day-to-day experience of discrimination. It is not surprising to find consistent discrepancies in health outcomes between "blacks" and "whites."

The physician Mary Bassett and the epidemiologist Nancy Krieger, looking at mortality risks from breast cancer, have found that the black/white differential of 1.35 drops to 1.10 when they look at African- and European-American women of comparable social class, as measured by a range of social indicators.[16] And within each "racial" group, social class is correlated with mortality risk. Because of racial oppression, being black is a predictor of increased health risks, but so is being poor, no matter what one's skin color may be. The fact that even at comparable education and class standing, some health risks appear to be greater for African than for European Americans needs to be analyzed by taking the range of factors into account that constitute the panorama of American racism.[17,18]

Our society's constructs of race differences, like those of sex differences, penetrate the biological sciences. When we use science to investigate subjects like race or sex, which are suffused with cultural meanings and embedded in power relationships, we need to be wary of scientific descriptions and interpretations that support, or even enhance, the prevailing political realities.

The same can be said about genes. DNA, the chemical, has material reality, but the concept of the gene, which long pre-dates any thought of DNA, has been constructed to fill a host of political, economic, and cultural as well as scientific needs. For this reason, we would do well to become suspicious whenever characteristics are attributed to genes that neatly fit these rather inert molecules for their ideological tasks.

The Social Practice of Science

A Review of *Primate Visions: Gender, Race, and Nature in the World of Modern Science* by Donna Haraway. New York: Routledge, 1989.

> The themes of race, sexuality, gender, nation, family, and class have been written into the body of nature in Western life sciences since the eighteenth century.

What is science? How is it produced? And what can it tell us about ourselves and the world? These are important questions in a time when everything from the structure of our genes to the quality of toothpaste are vouchsafed by science. Even anti-evolutionists, who try to challenge widely held scientific beliefs, do so by grounding their credo in a freshly minted "creation science." And both sides of the abortion debate cite scientists to support their arguments. That they can do this shows that science is not an "objective" rendering of "facts," but a social practice, subject to cultural and political norms.

Donna Haraway's book is about the social forces that go into constructing science and not only science, but our concepts of nature, the fabric scientists try to understand and describe. It is also about the ways both science and nature are embedded in history and culture, because the ways we perceive nature and relate to it are part of the process that lets us try to interpret it—be it religiously or scientifically.

Donna Haraway is a historian of science, trained as a biologist, who teaches in the History of Consciousness Program at the University of California at Santa Cruz. She is one of the more radical social constructionists who integrates how scientists see the world, the questions they ask about it, the means they employ to answer these questions, and the answers they find acceptable into a complex network of forces that include the scientists' institutional and professional support systems as well as their commitments as members of a nation, a culture, and of overlapping groups defined by race, class, gender, and sexual orientation

In this book, she tries to tease out how these interests and commitments are reflected in the stories scientists have been telling since the early years of this century about human origins and our primate ancestors. It is a densely woven fabric, at times almost too dense, but it is well worth sticking with her because what emerges is a picture that is broad in its sweep, yet full of articulated, specific detail. In ways deadly serious, yet funny, she shows us science as process and product, crafted by individuals, who not only belong to a race and class and gender, but who have faces, emotions, and relationships.

Haraway does not grant scientists the privilege to become detached, "objective" observers who exist outside their subject matter. She insists on naming the various ways in which they live inside the nature they describe and the ways in which their interpretations are structured by their culture and by power relationships that grow out of their race, class, gender, professional status, and national origin. Yet, always,

Haraway is a materialist. Science and nature may be socially constructed, but they are material and real. They do not dissolve in the social relations that structure the fields of vision and experience within which scientists discern and appraise them. The relationship between scientists and nature is played out within an on-going dialectic between observation and creation, invention and description, the terms of which are defined by the lives of these scientists as individuals and as members of the various overlapping groups of which they are part.

For Haraway science is not the stalwart effort to discover the "truth" about nature. For one thing, there is no unique, uncontestable truth to be had. What is "true" about nature depends on who is asking, under what historical and sociopolitical circumstances, from what point of view, and to what end. Western scientists are trained to look upon nature (including people) as a "resource" to dominate and exploit. In the context of capitalism and the never-ending quest for expanding markets, this has led us to the brink of ecological and nuclear disaster. Nature as resource, human beings as resources, are wrong metaphors and a science based on them is likely to come up with dangerous answers.

Early on, Haraway introduces two themes that are important throughout. One is the Western dichotomy between nature and culture, with animals, including monkeys and apes (and sometimes women) standing in for nature, while "man" represents culture. The other is the fact that for Euro-American scientists to study non-human primates, they must go to "Third World" countries that were colonies in the early days of primatology and are still regarded as

189

"resources" and not equals in the West. Haraway underlines this multi-faceted potential for exploitation from the start. Later she expands on it when she compares the research goals, techniques, and results of Western primatologists with those of their Japanese and Indian colleagues, who are differently situated in both respects. Since the Eastern religious and cultural beliefs and practices stress continuity between humans and animals, these scientists do not need to divide culture from nature; and also, they do not need to travel to foreign places to study non-human primates. Therefore, although a few scientists from these countries study African primates, apes and monkeys for them are not part of that return to the bosom of nature that has been such a powerful symbol for Western Man "alone" in darkest Africa.

The political realities of scientific practice—who becomes a scientist, how and under whose auspices she or he acquires the capability and permission to make authenticated facts, how one must formulate and communicate one's descriptions and interpretations—as well as the political and historical realities of the global and local systems within which primatologists (a necessarily well-traveled bunch) must operate are at the heart of the discussion. As a feminist, I am used to thinking about scientific descriptions of women's bodies as "maps of power" on which masculinist scientists have inscribed their stories, but Haraway broadens this now conventional feminist wisdom. She points out the ways the politics of racial, colonial, and neo-colonial domination have structured our views and knowledge not only of African peoples (something anti-racists and anti-colonialists have stressed), but of the non-human pri-

190

mates with whom they share the continent in which Western scientists have been trying to track our human origins. "The primate body," she writes, "may be read as a map of power.... [It] is an intriguing kind of political discourse.... Western primatology has been about the construction of the self from the raw material of the other, the appropriation of nature in the construction of culture.... Monkeys and apes mirror humans in a complex play of distortions over centuries of Western commentary...." (pp.10-11)

Like Evelyn Fox Keller, Haraway draws a parallel between the Western dualisms of nature and culture and sex and gender, in which nature and sex are as crafted as culture and gender are. Being an activist, she is explicit about the fact that one of the aims of the book is to explore how these dualisms can be disassembled in the interest of furthering equality and liberation.

Haraway uses striking pictures and powerful stories to make her points. For example, Chapter Three, entitled "Teddy Bear Patriarchy: Taxidermy in the Garden of Eden, New York City, 1908-36" is a riveting account of Carl Akeley's creation of the dioramas in the African Hall at the American Museum of Natural History in New York. With consummate skill she evokes Akeley's ambivalent pride in killing the most magnificent animals he can find in order to construct "typical" scenes of an African Eden. Here is Akeley describing the giant male gorilla he selected for the Hall: "As he lay at the base of the tree, it took all one's scientific ardour to keep from feeling like a murderer. He was a magnificent creature with the face of an amiable giant who would do no harm except perhaps in self defense or indefense of his family" (p.34). (Note Akeley's effort to distance himself. It took "*one's* scientific ardour," not his.) Akeley's vision of jungle peace "justified to himself his hunting, turned it into a tool of science and art, the scalpel that revealed the harmony of an organic, articulated world" (p.38). He killed the animals in the interest of speaking truth about nature.

Haraway won't let us forget the racism inherent in the recreation of life in the "wild," the jungle idyll. She quotes from a fund-raising prospectus prepared at Akeley's suggestion to support a photographic expedition about "African Babies" for the American Museum of Natural History: "It will show elephant babies, lion babies, zebra babies, giraffe babies, and black babies [!]...showing the play of wild animals and the maternal care that is so strange and inter.esting a feature of wild life" (p.45)

"Wild life" is observed and recorded by white men or women, "alone" in the jungle, surrounded by native porters and guides, who are nameless and don't count. In a remarkable footnote (p.387), which could be the outline for another book, Haraway summarizes various nineteenth-century expeditions by white women "alone" in Africa.

In recent times, such returns to "nature" have happened with more fanfare. "How do the race, species, gender, and science codes work to reinvent nature in the Third World for First World audiences within post-colonial, multinational capitalism?" she asks (p.135). The answer: By having the National Geographic Society prepare articles and film specials in which the white hand of a young woman-scientist (Jane Goodall) is gently enfolded in that of a hairy chimpanzee (under the sponsorship of the Gulf Oil

Corporation). Jane Goodall, Birute Galdikas, Dian Fossey—the first of quite a number of women scientists mediating "man's" understanding of "his" primate ancestry "in the wild" and the laboratory; white women teaching apes to speak in trailers in Silicon Valley and, more recently, teaching them how to survive in their "native" habitat, since they have become so few in number that each one returned "to the wild" counts.

Haraway's interweaving of the iconographies of "high science," science fiction, and popular science, as presented in films and magazines, makes fascinating reading. She writes: "Throughout *Primate Visions*, I have read both popular and technical discourses on monkeys and apes 'out of context.'... My hope has been that the always oblique and sometimes perverse focusing would facilitate revisionings of fundamental, persistent Western narratives about difference, especially racial and sexual difference; about reproduction...; and about survival..." (p.377). As the reader is led back and forth among scientific expeditions, field notes, popular films, laboratory experiments, histories of individual researchers, museum exhibits, all contextualized in political and historical time and space, it is sometimes hard to hold on to the story. But the common threads are there and always worth seeking out. The one thing I would criticize is that Haraway's language is needlessly difficult. Not all her readers will be familiar with the ways of modern literary criticism. She erects unnecessary barriers by requiring them, again and again, to translate "semiotics," "inscription devices," "tropes," "discursive fields," and the like into plain speech.

My other criticism—and I have only one other—

is that the book would benefit from an explicit discussion of what Haraway believes to be an appropriate role for science. She shows how embedded not just science, but also what we call nature, are in culture. But culture-laden or not, not all concepts of nature and not all scientific explanations and practices are equivalent, and Haraway expresses clear preferences. She thinks our understanding of primate behavior has been improved because scientists from Asia have entered the field, and considers it a detriment that so few professional primatologists are native to Africa, and that of those few, most are South African (and presumably white). It is clear also that she likes the ways Western women, who are feminists *and* scientists, have lately restructured what can count as evidence and explanation, and have recast the acceptable analyses and descriptions of primate behavior and social relationships.

Since what we believe about ourselves affects our notions of who we can be, and since these beliefs are influenced by what scientists tell us, how we think science operates is clearly important. That is what this book is about and why it is an important book. But in a book so full of descriptive detail and analysis, readers would benefit from having Haraway draw the strands of her argument together and perhaps also discuss what she thinks it would take to improve scientific practices and systems of explanation. That said, I can only urge you to read the book, to skim or skip when necessary, but to keep going. It is an important book that has a lot to teach us about our "nature," our history, and hopefully our survival individually and as a species, for as Haraway says: "Questions about the nature of war, technology, power, and community echo through the primate literature.... Reinvented [human] origins have been figures for reinvented possible futures" (p.369). Our future, and whether we have one, depend on how we negotiate the "cultural and political boundaries that separate and link animal, human, and machine in a contemporary global world where survival is at stake" (p.382).

Science and
Feminism

Comments on *Building Two-Way Streets: The Case of Feminism and Science* by Anne Fausto-Sterling

Before I retired from teaching in 1990, I used to offer a course at Harvard called "Biology and Women's Issues." Since students could get credit for it in either biology or women's studies, it drew a fairly mixed group of undergraduates from the natural and social sciences and the humanities, as well as, occasionally, graduate students from the Divinity School, the Schools of Education and Public Health, and even medical students.

Early on in the term, we usually went around the room and the students talked about why they were, or were not, majoring in the natural sciences. Again and again, women students would say that they had loved their science courses in high school and had come to college expecting to major in a natural science, but that in freshman chemistry or physics or math, they had found themselves outnumbered, ignored, and discouraged and had therefore shifted to psychology, history of science, or indeed literature where they felt more welcome. Occasionally, though much more rarely, a similar story was told by a man. And it was not that these students had lost their curiosity about nature or their interest in learning about it. They had just found the classes alienating. Among other problems, their curiosity and interest were stamped out by the plethora of facts, rules, formulas, and vocabulary they were expected to learn in the introductory courses.

This certainly was my own experience in my introductory science courses and the only reason I stuck with a science major was that I intended to become a physician. That I eventually went into science, not medicine, resulted from the near-accident that, during my last year in college, I started to work in an actual research laboratory where people were excited about their experiments. (In the September 1992 issue of the *Radcliffe Quarterly*, the alumnae newsletter, Radcliffe president Linda Wilson, a chemist by training, wrote proudly that 48.6 percent of the women admitted to the Harvard class of 1996 expressed an interest in science. I am glad, but wonder how many of them have ended up majoring in a science.)

The problem is not just the antithesis between women and science—an antithesis that certainly exists in our culture—but that much elementary science teaching consists in boring recitations of "facts" rather than in introducing students to the process of thinking up interesting scientific questions and figuring out how to answer them. Since women have an "out" in that they and science are thought not to go together, they often opt for more interesting and inviting disciplines.

There is another problem. Biologist Anne Fausto-Sterling has written of the pleasure she takes in "observing the natural world." I share that pleasure, but have long been troubled about the fact that, in our technological and urbanized society, the opportunity to observe "the natural world" has become a luxury to which few children, or indeed grown-ups, have access. It used to be that students came to science because, growing up, they had become interested in some particular aspects of nature and were curious to find out more about it. Now the reverse is true: increasing numbers of students come to nature through science. If they are lucky, kindergarten or first grade may expose them to a "science corner," with lush molds growing on old bread or potatoes, perhaps some gerbils trying to build a burrow out of shredded newspaper, or a frog or snake trying to survive in a terrarium while fish swim about in their one-gallon aquarium. If the children are even luckier, their parents or teachers will take them to see "wild animals" looking out from behind bars, or large fishes, turtles, or seals swimming in big tanks. Many an urban child never sees a plant or animal living "in nature." So, where is their curiosity and interest to come from?

I am lucky because I spend part of my time at the seashore, which is still relatively "natural" and full of plants and animals living their own lives. But I remember the astonishment of a young friend, who had grown up in Oakland, California, at seeing trees and bushes and grass growing in a marsh or in the woods—not a few of them in a carefully laid-out private garden or public park, but a whole bunch just growing.

It is not easy for a modern American child to develop an interest in understanding nature. People have got used to the idea that science is about obscure and not all that interesting phenomena, that it is full of difficult concepts and jargon, and that you have to be awfully smart to understand it. And many of them are not sure it is worth the trouble. A megaproject like the human genome project is being sold not by talking about its potential scientific interest. No, genome scientists and their allies promise that it will enable them to solve all imaginable human problems—cure diseases, improve intelligence, prevent crime, solve homelessness.

Indeed, it would help if greater numbers of feminists had the scientific training to see through the public relations gimmicks and the confidence to argue against putting resources into a project that rides on the dangerous ideology that our genes are responsible for all our personal and societal problems. But most of the time, scientific training is narrow and specialized and few of us feminists in science can be sure that we would have submitted to it had we come to feminism before we came to science, and had we been aware of the interesting ways of thinking about science that a feminist analysis opens up. It cannot be an accident that a number of us, who became scientists before we experienced the impact of feminist thinking, stopped doing science once we became interested in feminist analyses and began to develop feminist science studies.

One reason for this change in direction is that we found analyzing science more interesting than doing it. But another, and one whose force must not be underestimated, is that scientists do not welcome colleagues who ask questions about the social context in which their discipline has grown up or about the ways it is being practiced. They resent science scholars who point out that political and social and economic factors shape the ways scientists understand nature as well as the ways they establish priorities among the questions they consider worth asking about it.

By and large, feminists, who are both practicing scientists and intellectually stimulated by exploring the framework and workings of science, must keep their feminist and sociological interests in the closet. They may admit their "subversive" questions to close friends—even if these friends are scientists—but they cannot expect that their scientist-friends will share their sociological or historical curiosity. Young scientists aspiring to get tenure in one of the scientific disciplines are in a difficult position if they are also closeted disciples of the new feminist science studies. It is hard enough for a young woman to make her way in academic science, but a deviant has additional strikes against her.

Despite all that, it is important for feminists to develop an understanding of the bearing scientific and technological innovations have on our lives. The new molecular biology, including the medical technologies, tests, and pharmaceuticals that will be developed as a result of the genome initiative, are likely to have dramatic effects on procreation, education, employment and insurance practices, as well as on health care. This raises special responsibilities for those of us who live in both worlds. We must try to communicate the scientific findings and draw out their implications. It is true that non-specialists are all too ready to proclaim their lack of interest in the arcane intricacies of molecular biology. But the way molecular biologists communicate with each other also does not readily allow outsiders to understand them. Even papers published in journals like *Science*, which are supposed to be relatively accessible, are so filled with acronyms, jargon, and other unnecessary obfuscations as to turn away anyone who does not need to read them for professional reasons. To try to read papers published in more specialized, professional journals is quite hopeless.

In the humanities and social sciences, journal articles are usually written in a language outsiders can read, though increasingly these disciplines, too, are being isolated within walls of needless obfuscation. Fortunately, scholars in these disciplines still write books in addition to articles. And since book publishers need to generate a profit, even scholarly books must be at least somewhat readable.

For natural scientists, writing books is not an avenue of professional communication or advancement, though it used to be. At the beginning of this century, scientists still communicated their results in books as well as articles, and both were intended for a wider audience than their intimate colleagues and therefore written in plain English (or German or French). Only in recent decades have scientists resurrected the practice of communicating their discoveries in what might as well be medieval Latin.

To the extent that natural scientists write books, they mostly write them to translate and popularize the primary literature, though they usually delegate that task to science writers and other "secondary sources"—people who are engaged not in doing science, but in communicating its results. Few non-scientists are able to check to what extent such books reflect what scientists are actually doing or saying to each other. And unfortunately, the popularizers often write what is essentially advertising copy, like the "ain't science grand" books we used to be handed when we were children. This is dangerous for everyone, women and men, feminists and traditionalists.

Fausto-Sterling has pointed to the problem that women's studies scholars and feminists, in general, do not know enough about what is going on in the sciences, and that they acquiesce too readily in their scientific illiteracy and their ignorance about what natural scientists are thinking and doing. But I do not think this is due primarily to their unwarranted modesty or self-exclusion. Such ignorance is the consequence of well-developed processes of obfuscation on the one hand, and science salesmanship on the other. I take it to be one of the tasks of those of us who are engaged in feminist science studies to translate and interpret science and to help people identify the exclusionary practices. Then feminists can protest such practices, as we have protested other attempts at shutting us out, rather than accept that, because we are women, science simply is not for us and we don't need to know anything about it.

In a Science Restructured Along Feminist Lines,

Would the Laws of Gravity No Longer Hold?

Though we see the same world, we
see it through different eyes.

Virginia Woolf,
Three Guineas

The feminist insights that have resulted in restructuring knowledge in the humanities and social sciences have hardly touched the natural sciences. Even at my own university, which is not known to be at the forefront of the feminist revolution, the *Harvard Crimson* has complained that too few faculty members in the English department were versed in feminist scholarship to make the department attractive to graduate students. A similar situation would be unthinkable in the sciences.[1]

The reason is that scientists (meaning natural scientists) believe that they simply render nature as it is. They equate science with nature, or the closest approximation to it that they can technically achieve, because they believe that what we call nature, as well as the scientific processes of investigating it, are universal and independent of human history and culture. Scientists, they believe, try to come as close as they can to rendering nature and they do so objectively, that is, irrespective of their personal or cultural commitments. The degree to which they succeed in comprehending nature and making it comprehensible to others determines the quality of their scientific work—whether it is good or bad science.

In contrast, I would answer the question with which I entitle this essay by saying that in a feminist universe apples will indeed continue to fall, unless someone throws them up in the air, but this does not mean that all attempts to understand this reality scientifically would necessarily produce the laws of gravity as we know them.

The point is that both nature and the sciences that try to explicate it are cultural constructs that operate for specific purposes and serve the contexts in which they are produced. This is not to deny that nature exists; but our conceptions of it, even prior to any conscious effort at description or explanation, necessarily are interpretations, and embedded in history and culture.[2]

Scientific Objectivity

That scientists have difficulty understanding this situation is due to their belief that the methodology of science ensures objectivity. Scientific experimentation and verification, they argue, are accessible to anyone and results are "true" only to the extent that they can be replicated and shared by whoever wishes to try. Therefore, there can be no question of subjectivity or cultural bias. One way they achieve this illusion of universality is by erasing the scientist/agent and reporting their observations in phrases that begin with "It has been observed that..." or "It will be seen that...."

I agree that subjectivity and bias can be reduced within the limited context of a scientific experiment, whose questions and parameters are precisely defined and isolated from the wider world in which the scientists and their experiments are situated. But objectivity, so defined, cannot guard against the biases and commitments shared by substantial interest groups, and it can avoid them even less if these commitments are shared by the entire culture. This is why reputable nineteenth-century biologists were able to "prove" that the brains of women and of African American men were smaller than those of Euro-American males and how Arthur Jensen in 1969 was able to "prove" that the IQ of African Americans is lower than that of Americans of European descent.[3]

Feminists recognize that subjectivity is unavoidable. To acknowledge it enhances our ability to appraise our relationship to the objects and people among whom we live and work. Not only is the personal political, but it informs all our thoughts and actions. We can deny our subjectivity only by ignoring it, because we cannot eliminate it. This realization puts us at odds with scientists who make objectivity a cornerstone of what they believe about their method of investigation. But in science, as elsewhere, objectivity exists in dynamic, dialectical tension with subjectivity. If anything, it would be enhanced to the extent that scientists acknowledged their social, philosophical, personal, and other locations relative to the objects they study.

Since scientists are a rather homogeneous

group—predominantly European or Euro-American, male, upper-middle-class—and have passed through an educational process that has taught them to look at the world in specific ways, their so-called objectivity is enclosed within their shared commitments. Only by ignoring these limitations can a distinguished scientist, like my Harvard colleague E.O. Wilson, open the last chapter of his *Sociobiology: The New Synthesis*, which deals with human nature and social relationships, with the words: "Let us now consider man in the free spirit of natural history, as though we were zoologists from another planet completing a catalog of social species on earth."[4] This statement implies not only that there is a "free spirit of natural history," but that earthly zoologists can look upon their fellow-human beings, whom Wilson with due objectivity calls "man," as though they were "zoologists from another planet," which planet would of course have developed the same academic disciplines as Western societies.

Small wonder that the "human nature" Wilson projects is characterized by personality traits that make for success in modern capitalist societies and by gender differences that can provide achievement-oriented men with stay-at-home wives to care for these men and their children. I do not want to belabor the issue, except to point out that the fact that a distinguished scientist can offer such value-laden descriptions illustrates the apparent naïveté and ideological biases, which are among the barriers that a feminist restructuring of science will need to overcome.

Dialectical tensions between objectivity and subjectivity are inherent in feminist as well as in scientific scholarship and have been explored by

Sandra Harding[5] and others. These scholars have also begun to call attention to the systematic explorations of nature indigenous to Africa, Asia, and the so-called New World, and to the fact that these explorations have been obscured by Euro-American domination in science as well as in politics.[6] Critics of Western science must begin to collect concrete examples of different, ordered, systematic ways of viewing and explaining nature, and that have yielded the kinds of useful knowledge that Western scientists believe arise uniquely from our way of understanding nature through science. I shall come back to this point in a little while with reference to women's traditional ways of exploring nature.

Feminist analysts and critics of science such as Carolyn Merchant and Evelyn Fox Keller have described the ways in which Western science has transformed nature from an organism into a machine, and how the transformations in ideology that accompanied the technical innovations through which nature has been made available for large-scale use and exploitation have introduced gender metaphors, so that nature has become feminine and science masculine.[7,8] Such formulations have not entered the scientific mainstream. As with objectivity and subjectivity, a chasm still yawns between scientific and feminist views about science and nature. To the extent that conventional scientists know of the feminist analyses, they tend to brush them aside as sociology or philosophy or history of science and as irrelevant to scientific practice. They certainly do not acknowledge them as necessary to a more comprehensive, and hopefully less domineering and destructive, understanding of nature.

Animal Behavior and Human Origins

Against this bleak backdrop, it is interesting that there are two areas in which feminist thinking has, in fact, changed scientific descriptions and explanations—the study of animal behavior and of human origins. Here a rich literature has developed in which feminist reappraisals have made a difference. So let us look at this point of light, lest my entire discussion be cast in gloom.

In 1948 Ruth Herschberger caricatured the standard experimental approaches of sex differences research and the resulting descriptions of primate behavior.[9] But her delightful book got little notice until it was resurrected in the 1970s, when feminist biologists, anthropologists, and historians of science began to recast the standard descriptions of animal behavior and of evolution and primate and human origins. In "Have Only Men Evolved?" I questioned Darwin's theory of sexual selection, which was based on the assumption that males are always in competition with each other for sexual access to all available females, while the females stand by and wait to go off with the winner.[10] As we saw earlier, according to this formulation, males are therefore said to have evolved to be aggressive and competitive, females coy and choosy. In the same essay, I also called attention to the various gender assumptions underlying contemporary descriptions of animal behavior and of human origins. Book-length discussions of these topics by Sarah Blaffer Hrdy, Nancy Tanner, and others have since changed these fields.[11,12] Recently, Donna Haraway has broadened the analysis by looking not only at underlying assumptions about gender, but also at assumptions about race, class, and colonized/colonizer status that have been incorporated into standard thinking about primate origins and behavior.[13]

In an interesting essay, Hrdy has reflected on the process by which she came to question the descriptions of primate behavior she had accepted as a student and young researcher while watching monkeys in the field.[14] She argues that, in the standard male-centered accounts, "no conscious effort was made to leave...female sides to stories" out of the descriptions (p. 127), but simply no one ever troubled to look at what the females were actually doing. And she attributes the shift in focus introduced by female researchers, including herself, to their "empathy for other females" (p. 120). While I am uncomfortable with this entirely individualistic explanation that does not acknowledge the cultural and professional contexts in which scientists make their observations and formulate their explanations, this is an astonishing admission to come from a scientist who is in the mainstream of her field and, on the whole, not critical of the ordinary processes by which science is made. It suggests that scientists who study animal behavior are open to exploring the dynamic interrelations of subjectivity and objectivity which go into the initial process of making observations and into the subsequent attempts to abstract and generalize from them.

Reductionism and Hierarchy

This kind of openness to the possibility that feminist insights have something important to contribute is not shared by scientists who study the "hard" sciences, the sciences that consist of taking the objects of daily experience apart into smaller and smaller units, and eventually into "ultimate" particles.

It is a good question why, in the hierarchy of scientific fields and knowledge, the more abstract and intangible the objects under investigation, the higher the status of the field. That is what puts mathematics and the most mathematicized fields, such as theoretical physics and particle physics, at the top of the hierarchy. It is also what gives reductionism its high status, because reductionism is based on the assumption that to understand the world, we must take it apart into smaller and smaller bits. The claim is that only when we understand those bits will we be able to figure out how the whole thing works. This way of looking at the world ignores the dialectical transformations that connect the parts with the whole. The fact is that we cannot, for example, deduce how cells function by studying the molecules inside them any more than we can predict how a society will function by studying the individuals who live in it.

It is also a good question why knowledge has to be arranged into a hierarchy altogether. Nature is not hierarchical, but the societies in which our kind of science is made are. This is presumably why, though hierarchy is not inherent in nature, we speak of higher and lower organisms as well as inventing a hierarchy of disciplines. But that does not explain why the more abstract sciences have the greatest prestige. I would guess that that has something to do with the differential valuing by Western culture of the body and the mind and of mental and manual labor.

Clearly, in a world full of real, everyday needs

and of equally real dangers that grow out of short-sighted pursuits of science and technology, we must reappraise the intellectual and social frameworks that have led to considering the pursuit of increasingly rarefied realms of scientific knowledge to be an unquestioned good. To say this is heresy among my scientific colleagues, but as feminists and people concerned about human survival, we need to face this issue.

Knowledge and Experience

The Canadian feminist and metallurgist Ursula Franklin has argued that the problem with science is that it separates knowledge from experience.[15] She goes on to say that that kind of practice may be all right in astronomy, where our tangible experience is necessarily minimal, but that it is dangerous when we apply it to more daily realms of experience. Turning certain aspects of daily experience into knowledge distorts our experiences because it renders those aspects abstract and unreal.

I was introduced to botany and zoology in college without ever having consciously seen an animal or plant be born, develop and grow, get old, and die. I was introduced to abstractions about genes, which at that time in scientific history were quasi-mathematical concepts devoid of material reality, before I had any experience of the richness and diversity of organic life. This may be a small example and perhaps a less dangerous one than some. Yet I could have accepted (and no doubt did accept) all kinds of destructive ways of thinking about animals and plants. I was quite ready to manipulate plants without trying to integrate what I learned about them with the realities of seeds, soils, and daily labor, or to dissect pickled animals without thinking about how they had lived and died.

Women's traditional knowledge has been embedded in daily realities and labors, and has been inextricable from experience. But, as Ursula Franklin also points out, the radical cleavage of knowledge from experience can make science seem bloodless and abstract, hence often uninteresting to girls and minority children of both sexes whose lives usually are suffused with dailyness. In addition, it downgrades the kinds of knowledge that are intimately tied to experience. Women's traditional knowledge has not been granted the status of science, since science is knowledge abstracted from its origins in daily practice. As I said earlier, science is considered to be at its best and "hardest" when it mathematicizes nature or, at least, conceptualizes it as broken up into bits devoid of experiential counterparts. The nature described by the "softer" sciences can sometimes still be touched, but usually not by "real" scientists, only by the people who get their hands dirty, the so-called technicians. This radical division of knowledge from experience lends itself to the easy use of science for disfigurement, dismemberment, and destruction. And that is true of peaceful uses of science in agriculture or medicine as well as of its frankly destructive uses for war.

In *The Politics of Women's Biology* I have written about some models of a science more grounded in experience. I cited the women's health movement as an example, because here women have gotten together and, by comparing their experiences and checking them against the scientific descriptions, have tried to get a better understanding of the ways our bodies function. I also suggested that the knowledge women have traditionally gathered in their gardens, kitchens, and sickrooms needs to be acknowledged as scientific. A group of Canadian women have published a series of articles in which they do just that by elaborating on the scientific content of domestic agriculture, food science, and the care of birthing women and of sick people.[16]

Karen Messing, a geneticist and feminist at the University of Quebec, has described the problems she and her colleagues have faced when they want to answer questions that grow out of people's daily experience, such as the work practices of female and male workers.[17] These researchers have encountered not only the obvious problems of funding, which in Messing's case has been made easier by an agreement between her university and the two major trade unions in the province of Quebec, but have also found scientists at other institutions less than cooperative. The work Messing and her colleagues are doing is often not considered "real science." For example, they are trying to answer questions about possible genetic damage, produced by exposure to radiation in the workplace, by consulting and examining the people who are directly affected and interested to know the answers because they work there. Yet, more traditional scientists have told Messing that the results would be more valid if she and her colleagues used animal models or isolated cells, and then extrapolated their observations to the presumed experiences of imaginary workers.

The point is that scientists are unwilling to accept feminist insights and methods not only because of traditional gender biases, but also because feminist knowledge tends to be grounded in practice, since feminists are reluctant to separate theory and practice, head and hand. The kinds of decontextualized and alienated knowledge science offers is hard to reconcile with feminist principles, whereas scientists are not eager to acknowledge the contextual location of their work and its inevitable impact on the political and personal realities of people's lives. They tend to touch on real-life implications of their research only when they engage in public relations and wish to highlight the benefits it might yield.

What's to Be Done?

As feminists, we cannot accept the idea that all knowledge is equally worth pursuing. What is more, we must insist on democratic mechanisms whereby people other than the scientists doing the work can get involved in decisions about what needs to be done. Such choices must be made on the basis of social utility, not of prestige or profit. Scientists always make choices; but they pretend that their choices are driven by the internal logic of their subject and by the free play of their educated curiosity. Yet it is dangerous to ignore the contextual framework that shapes their subject matter, their curiosity, and their choices.

Given that feminists are not content to study the world, but want to change it, what can we do to bridge the chasm I have described? We must rally our natural allies—the women and men who not only feel threatened by the scientific and technological practices that surround us, but who do not see any

216

prospect of influencing or even understanding them. The prevailing mystification of science and technology is quite unnecessary. Ordinary people need to be able to feel pride in the knowledge and experience they accumulate in their daily lives and not always feel overshadowed by so-called experts. Those of us who are educators must make our training and skills available—and often for translation more than instruction—so that a wider range of people can participate in the process of making and distributing the knowledge that grows out of their daily experience.

Feminists in universities are in a privileged position as long as we remain grounded in the women's movement and the women's community (or rather, communities), because we can then serve as bridges between the university and our communities. Most academic scientists have outside ties only with corporate business and with government agencies, but not with community groups, whether these are organized around health or environmental issues, consumer interests, or conditions of work (such as trade unions). By contrast, I am suggesting that we must ground scientific inquiry in the needs and questions of ordinary people, if science is to be understandable and useful. This may seem a daunting task, but we must take it on if we want to help make scientists partners in a democratic enterprise. And as feminists we cannot afford to settle for less.

Notes and References

Predictive Genetics and the Construction of the Healthy Ill

1. Mary Midgley. *Science as Salvation: A Modern Myth and Its Meaning.* London and New York: Routledge, 1992, p.190.

2. Leo Tolstoy. *The Death of Ivan Ilyich.* [1886] New York: Bantam Books, 1981.

3. Rainer Maria Rilke. *The Notebooks of Malte Laurids Brigge.* [1910] New York: Random House, 1983.

4. Sylvia Noble Tesh. *Hidden Arguments: Political Ideology and Disease Prevention Policy.* New Brunswick, New Jersey: Rutgers University Press, 1988.

5. Thomas McKeown. *The Modern Rise of Population.* New York: Academic Press, 1976.

6. Tesh. *Hidden Arguments,* p.35.

7. Dolores Kong. "Age-old illnesses making comeback." *Boston Globe,* September 9, 1991, pp. 41 & 46.

8. Rayna Rapp. "Chromosomes and communication: the discourse of genetic counseling." In Linda M. Whitford and Marilyn L. Polant, eds. *New Approaches to Human Reproduction: Social and Ethical Dimensions.* Boulder, Colorado: Westview Press, 1989, pp. 25–41.

9. Shelly R. Miller and Robert H. Schwartz. "Attitudes toward genetic testing of Amish, Mennonite, and Hutterite families with cystic fibrosis." *American Journal of Health,* vol. 82, pp. 236–242, 1992.

10. Rapp, p. 36.

11. Rapp, p. 30.

12. Dorothy C. Wertz, Sally R. Janes, Janet M. Rosenfield, and Richard W. Erbe. "Attitudes toward the prenatal diagnosis of cystic fibrosis: Factors in decision making among affected families." *American Journal of Human Genetics,* vol. 50, pp. 1077–1085, 1992.

13. Jeffrey R. Botkin and Sonia Alemagno. "Carrier screening for cystic fibrosis: a pilot study of the attitudes of pregnant

     women." *American Journal of Public Health*, vol. 82, pp. 723–725, 1992.

14. Wertz et al., p. 1082.

15. Hannah Arendt coined this pithy phrase in her summing up of the Eichmann trial. See Hannah Arendt. *Eichmann in Jerusalem: A Report on the Banality of Evil*. New York: Penguin Books, 1977, p. 279.

16. E.H. Corder, A.M. Sauders, W.J. Strittmatter, D.E. Schmechel, P.C. Gaskell, G.W. Small, A.D. Roses, J.L. Haines, and M.A. Pricak-Vance. "Gene dose of apolipoprotein E Type 4 allele and the risk of Alzheimer's disease in late onset families." *Science*, vol. 261, pp. 921–923, 1993.

17. John Travis. "New piece in Alzheimer's puzzle." *Science*, vol. 261, pp. 828–829, 1993.

18. Associated Press. "Study Suggests Tests Can Predict Alzheimer's." *New York Times*, August 30, 1994.

19. Ruth Hubbard and Elijah Wald. *Exploding the Gene Myth*. Boston: Beacon Press, 1993, chapter 9.

20. Paul Billings and Ruth Hubbard. "Fragile X Testing: Who Benefits?" *Genewatch*, vol. 8, no. 3–4, pp. 1–3, January 1994.

21. Paul Billings, Mel Kohn, Marguerite de Cuevas, Jon Beckwith, Joseph S. Alper, and Marvin R. Natowicz. "Discrimination as a consequence of genetic testing." *American Journal of Human Genetics*, vol. 50, pp. 476–482, 1992.

22. Dorothy Nelkin and Laurence Tancredi. *Dangerous Diagnostics: The Social Power of Biological Information*, 2nd edition. Chicago, IL: University of Chicago Press, 1994, especially chapter 6.

23. Larry Gostin. "Genetic discrimination: The use of genetically based diagnostic and prognostic tests by employers and insurers." *American Journal of Law and Medicine*, vol. 17, pp. 109–144, 1991.

24. Joseph S. Alper and Marvin R. Natowicz. "Genetic discrimination and the public entities and public accommodation titles of the Americans with Disabilities Act." *American Journal of Human Genetics*, vol. 53, pp. 26–32, 1993.

25. Hubbard and Wald. *Exploding the Gene Myth*. Boston, MA: Ch. 10.

Notes and References

26. No author. "Insurance task force makes recommendations." *Human Genome News*, vol. 5, no. 2, July 1993, pp. 1–2.

27. Janet C. Hoeffel. "The dark side of DNA profiling: Unreliable scientific evidence meets the criminal defendant." *Stanford Law Review*, vol. 42, pp. 465–538, 1990.

28. Paul R. Billings, ed. *DNA on Trial: Genetic Identification and Criminal Justice.* Cold Spring Harbor, N.Y.: Cold Spring Harbor Press, 1992, esp. pp. 119–149.

29. Walter Gilbert. "A vision of the grail." In Daniel J. Kevles and Leroy Hood, eds. *The Code of Codes: Scientific and Social Issues in the Human Genome Project.* Cambridge: Harvard University Press, 1992, pp. 83–97 (p. 84).

Transparent Women, Visible Genes and New Conceptions of Disease

1. Barbara Duden. *Disembodying Women: Perspectives on Pregnancy and the Unborn.* Cambridge, Massachusetts: Harvard University Press, 1993, chapter 2.

2. Duden, p. 12.

3. Walter Gilbert. "A Vision of the Grail," p. 96.

4. A.R. Luria. *The Making of Mind: A Personal Account of Soviet Psychology.* (Edited by Michael Cole and Sheila Cole). Cambridge: Harvard University Press, 1979, pp. 176–177.

5. Troy Duster. *Backdoor to Eugenics.* New York: Routledge, 1990.

Genes and Behavior

1. Philip Elmer-Devitt. "The Genetic Revolution." *Time*, January 17, 1994, pp. 46–53.

2. Matthew P. Dumont. *Treating the Poor: A Personal Sojourn through the Rise and Fall of Community Mental Health.* Belmont, MA: Dympha Press, 1992, p. 28. .

3. Ajita Chakraborty. "Culture, colonialism, and psychiatry." *Lancet* 337:1204–1207, 1991. .

4. Glyn Lewis et al. "Schizophrenia and city life." *Lancet* 340:137–140, 1992. .

5. David Cohen and Henri Cohen. "Biological Theories, Drug Treatments, and Schizophrenia: A Critical Assessment."

Journal of Mind and Behavior 7:11–35, 1986.

6. David E. Comings et al. "The Dopamine D2 Receptor Locus as a Modifying Gene in Neuropsychiatric Disorders." *Journal of the American Medical Association* 266:1793–1800, 1991; but see also Joel Gelenter et al. "No Association Between an Allele at the D2 Dopamine Receptor Gene (DRD2) and Alcoholism." Ibid., pp. 1801–1807.

7. Simon LeVay. "A Difference in Hypothalamic Structure Between Heterosexual and Homosexual Men." *Science* 253:1034–1037, 1991; but see also Anne Fausto-Sterling. *Myths of Gender: Biological Theories about Women and Men,* 2nd edition. New York: Basic Books, 1992, chapter 8.

8. Robin Sherrington et al. "Localization of a susceptibility locus for schizophrenia on chromosome 5." *Nature* 336: 164–167, 1988; but see also James L. Kennedy et al. "Evidence against linkage of schizophrenia to markers on chromosome 5 in a northern Swedish pedigree." Ibid., pp. 167–169.

9. See, for example, Dean H. Hamer et al. "A Linkage Between DNA Markers on the X Chromosome and Male Sexual Orientation." *Science* 261:321–327, 1993.

10. Michel Foucault. *Madness and Civilization: A History of Insanity in the Age of Reason.* New York: Random House, 1965.

11. Temple Grandin and Margaret M. Scariano. *Emergence: Labeled Autistic.* Novato, California: Arena Press, 1986.

12. Donna Williams. *Nobody Nowhere: The Extraordinary Autobiography of an Autistic.* New York: Times Books, 1992.

13. Susanna Kaysen. *Girl, Interrupted.* New York: Random House, 1993.

14. Kate Millett. *The Loony-Bin Trip.* New York: Simon and Schuster, 1990.

15. D.L. Rosenhan. "On Being Sane in Insane Places." *Science* 179: 250–258, 1973.

16. Gina Kolata. "Cystic Fibrosis Surprise: Genetic Screening Falters." *New York Times,* November 16, 1993, pp. C1, C3.

17. Elizabeth Culotta and Daniel E. Koshland, Jr. "p53 Sweeps Through Cancer Research." *Science* 262:1958–61, 1993.

18. Harold Erickson. *Journal of Cell Biology* 120:1079–1081, 1993.

19. Yukimo Saga et al. "Mice develop normally without tenascin." *Genes and Development* 6:1821–1831, 1992.
20. Patricia A. Jacobs et al. "Aggressive Behaviour, Mental Subnormality and the XYY Male." *Nature* 208:1351–1352, 1965.

Canceling a Conference on "Genetics and Crime"

1. R.C. Lewontin. *Biology as Ideology: The Doctrine of DNA.* New York: Harper Perennial, 1991, p. 33.

Sexism and Sociobiology

1. For a discussion of the interplay of some of these elements, see Mary Roth Walsh, *Doctors Wanted: No Women Need Apply* (New Haven: Yale University Press, 1977), pp. 133–137.
2. Cited in Walsh, *Doctors Wanted*, pp. 120–121.
3. Edward H. Clarke, *Sex in Education; or, a Fair Chance for the Girls* (Boston: James R. Osgood & Co., 1874).
4. Walsh, *Doctors Wanted*, pp. 120–121.
5. Clarke, *Sex in Education*, pp. 17–18.
6. Ibid., p. 16.
7. Ibid., p. 38.
8. Ibid., p. 39.
9. Ibid.
10. Walsh, *Doctors Wanted*, p. 129.
11. Eliza Bizbee Duffey, *No Sex in Education; or, an equal chance for both girls and boys* (Syracuse, 1874), cited in Walsh, *Doctors Wanted*, p. 128.
12. "Committee Report, Harvard Medical School," 1944, p. 2, Harvard Medical School Dean's Records, cited in Walsh, *Doctors Wanted*, p. 232.
13. Edward O. Wilson, *Sociobiology: The New Synthesis* (Cambridge, MA: Harvard University Press, 1975), p. 553.
14. Edward O. Wilson, "Human Decency is Animal," *New York Times Magazine*, October 12, 1975.
15. Edward O. Wilson, *On Human Nature* (Cambridge, MA: Harvard University Press, 1978) p. 133.

16. Wilson, *On Human Nature*, p. 126.
17. Wilson, *Sociobiology*, p. 4.
18. Wilson, *On Human Nature*, p. 169.
19. Ibid., p. 172.
20. Wilson, *Sociobiology*, p. 317.
21. Wilson, *On Human Nature*, p. 169.
22. Ibid., p. 147.
23. Ibid., p.124.
24. Ibid., p. 133.
25. Ibid., p. 89.
26. Ibid., p. 47.
27. Ibid., p. 190.
28. Anne Fausto-Sterling, *Myths of Gender: Biological Theories About Women and Men* (New York: Basic Books, 1986).
29. Wilson, *Sociobiology*, p. 547.
30. Margaret Mead, *Male and Female: A Study of the Sexes in a Changing World* (New York: Dell, 1949).

Which Facts? Whose Life?

1. Rayna Rapp. "Constructing Amniocentesis: Maternal and Medical Discourses." In *Uncertain Terms: Negotiating Gender in American Culture.* Faye Ginsburg and Anna Lowenhaupt Tsing, eds. Boston: Beacon Press, 1990, p. 28.

The Politics of Fetal/Maternal Conflict

Bertin, J.E. 1993. "Pregnancy and social control." In *Encyclopedia of Childbearing: Critical Perspectives.* B.K. Rothman, ed., pp. 317–323.

Billings, P., M. Kohn, M. de Cuevas, J. Beckwith, J.S. Alper, and M.R. Natowicz. 1992. "Discrimination as a consequence of genetic testing." *American Journal of Human Genetics* 50:476–482.

Bingol, N., C. Schuster, M. Fuchs, S. Iosub, G. Turner, R.K. Stone, and D.S. Gromisch. 1987. "The influence of socioeconomic factors on the occurrence of fetal alcohol syndrome." *Advances in Alcohol and Substance Abuse* (Special Issue: Children of Alcoholics) 6:105–118.

Notes and References

Blakeslee, S. 1991. "Research on birth defects turns to flaws in sperm." *New York Times*, January 1, p. 1.

Bowes, W.A., Jr. and B. Selegstad. 1981. "Fetal versus maternal rights: medical and legal perspectives." *Obstetrics and Gynecology* 58:209–214.

Chavkin, W. 1990. "Drug addiction and pregnancy: Policy crossroads." *American Journal of Public Health* 80:483–487.

Cole, H.M. 1990. "Legal interventions during pregnancy: Court-ordered medical treatments and legal penalties for potentially harmful behavior by pregnant women." *Journal of the American Medical Association* 264:2663–2670.

Florida v. Johnson. 1989. Case No. E89-890-CFA, Seminole County Circuit Court. July 13.

Hogue, C.J.R. and M.A. Hargraves. 1993. "Class, race, and infant mortality in the United States." *American Journal of Public Health* 83:9–12.

In re: *A.C., Appellant.* 1990. District of Columbia Court of Appeals No. 87–609, pp. 1105–1159.

International Union, UAW v. Johnson Controls. 1991. U.S. Supreme Court, No. 89–1215. March 20.

Kolata, G. 1990. "Racial bias seen on pregnant addicts." *New York Times*, July 20, p. A-13.

Kolder, V.E.B., J. Gallagher, and M.T. Parsons. 1987. "Court-ordered obstetrical interventions." *New England Journal of Medicine* 316:1192–1196.

Lieberman, J.R., M. Mazor, W. Chaim, and A. Cohen. 1979. "The fetal right to live." *Obstetrics and Gynecology* 53:515–517.

McNamara, E. 1989. "Fetal endangerment cases on the rise." *Boston Globe*, October 3, p. 1.

Moss, K.L. 1990. "Legal issues: Drug testing of postpartum women and newborns as the basis for civil and criminal proceedings." *Clearinghouse Review* 23:1406–1414.

Robertson, J.A. 1983. "Procreative liberty and the control of conception, pregnancy, and childbirth." *Virginia Law Review* 69:405–464.

Rothman, B.K. 1989. *The Tentative Pregnancy: Ideology and Technology in a Patriarchal Society.* New York: Norton.

Shriner, T.L. 1979. "Maternal rights versus fetal rights — a clinical dilemma." *Obstetrics and Gynecology* 53:518–519.

Slutsker, L., R. Smith, G. Higginson, and D. Fleming. 1993. "Recognizing illicit drug use by pregnant women: Reports from Oregon birth attendants." *American Journal of Public Health* 83:61–64.

Of Genies and Bottles: Technology, Values, and Choices

1. E.P. Thompson. *The Making of the English Working Class.* N.Y.: Vintage Books, 1966, p. 548

2. Ibid., p. 549

3. Hubbard and Wald. *Exploding the Gene Myth*, chapter 10.

Gender Ideology and the Biology of Sex Difference

1. Joseph Needham, "Human Law and the Laws of Nature," in Joseph Needham, *The Grand Titration* (London: Allen and Unwin, 1969).

2. Edward O. Wilson, *Sociobiology: The Modern Synthesis* (Cambridge: Harvard University Press, 1975).

3. Sarah Blaffer Hrdy, "Empathy, Polyandry, and the Myth of the Coy Female," in Ruth Bleier, ed., *Feminist Approaches to Science* (New York: Pergamon Press, 1986).

4. Anne Fausto-Sterling, "Society Writes Biology/Biology Constructs Gender," *Daedalus* 116: 61–76, 1987.

5. Diana Long Hall, "Biology, Sex Hormones, and Sexism in the 1920s," in Carol C. Gould and Marx W. Wartofsky, eds., *Women and Philosophy: Toward a Theory of Liberation* (New York: G.P. Putnam's Sons, 1976).

6. Emily Martin, "The Egg and the Sperm," *Signs* 16: 485–501, 1991.

7. David C. Page et al., "The Sex-Determining Region of the Human Y Chromosome Encodes a Finger Protein," *Cell* 51: 1091–1104, 1987.

8. M.S. Palmer et al., "Genetic evidence that ZFY is not the testis-determining factor," *Nature* 342: 937–939, 1989; Peter Koopman et al. "ZFY gene expression patterns are not compatible with a primary role in mouse sex determination," *Nature* 342: 940–942, 1989.

9. Natalie Angier, "Biologists Hot on Track of Gene for Femaleness," *New York Times*, August 30, 1994, C-1.

Constructs of Race Difference

1. Londa Schiebinger, *The Mind Has No Sex? Women and the Origins of Modern Science* (Cambridge: Harvard University Press, 1989), p. 165.

2. Allan Chase, *The Legacy of Malthus: The Social Costs of the New Scientific Racism* (New York: Alfred Knopf, 1977).

3. Stephen Jay Gould, *The Mismeasure of Man* (New York: W.W. Norton, 1981), p. 35.

4. Walter Rodney, *How Europe Underdeveloped Africa* (Dar-es-Salaam: Tanzania Publishing House, 1972), pp. 99–100.

5. Gould, p. 1036

6. Cited in Dorothy Burnham, "Black Women as Producers and Reproducers for Profit," in Marian Lowe and Ruth Hubbard, eds., *Woman's Nature: Rationalizations of Inequality* (New York: Pergamon Press, 1983), p.35.

7. Gunnar Myrdal, *An American Dilemma: The Negro Problem and Modern Democracy* (New York: Harper and Brothers, 1944), p. 1367.

8. Howard Zinn, *A People's History of the United States* (New York: Harper and Row, 1980), p. 406.

9. Leo Kuper, ed., *Race, Science and Society* (Paris: The UNESCO Press, 1975).

10. R.C. Lewontin, Steven Rose, and Leon J. Kamin, *Not In Our Genes: Biology, Ideology, and Human Nature* (New York: Pantheon, 1984), esp. pp. 119–129.

11. Richard Lewontin, *Human Diversity* (New York: Scientific American Books, 1982).

12. Janet L. Norwood and Deborah P. Klein, "Developing statistics to meet society's needs," *Monthly Labor Review* October 1989.

13. Ibid.

14. Ibid.

15 Nancy Krieger and Mary Bassett, "The Health of Black Folk: Disease, Class, and Ideology in Science," *Monthly Review* 38 (July–August 1986): 74–85 (74).

16. Mary T. Bassett and Nancy Krieger, "Social Class and Black-White Differences in Breast Cancer Survival," *American Journal of Public Health* 76 (1986): 1400–1403.

17. Kenneth C. Schoendorf, Carol J.R. Hogue, Joel C. Kleinman, and Diane Rowley, "Mortality among infants of black as compared with white college-educated parents," *New England Journal of Medicine* 326: 1522–1526, 1992.

18. For an attempt to initiate this sort of global analysis, see Nancy Krieger et al., "Racism, sexism, and social class: Implications for studies of health, disease, and well-being," *American Journal of Preventive Medicine* 9 (Supplement 2): 82–122, 1993.

In a Science Restructured Along Feminist Lines, Would the Laws of Gravity No Longer Hold?

1. I am using the conventional short-hand of calling the natural sciences "the sciences," because that is what most people call them; but it might not be bad to adopt the German system in which all ordered knowledge is science (Wissenschaft) and we need to specify the different branches of it—literary, historical, natural, etc.

2. I discuss this more fully in *The Politics of Women's Biology* (New Brunswick: Rutgers University Press, 1990).

3. Arthur R. Jensen, "How Much Can We Boost IQ and Scholastic Achievement?" *Harvard Educational Review* 39 (Winter): 1–123, 1969.

4. Edward O. Wilson, *Sociobiology: The New Synthesis* (Cambridge: Harvard University Press, 1975), p. 547.

5. Sandra Harding, *The Science Question in Feminism* (Ithaca: Cornell University Press, 1985).

6. Sandra Harding, ed., *The Racial Economy of Science: Toward a Democratic Future* (Bloomington, Indiana: Indiana University Press, 1993).

7. Carolyn Merchant, *The Death of Nature* (San Francisco: Harper and Row, 1980).

8. Evelyn Fox Keller, *Reflections on Gender and Science* (New Haven: Yale University Press, 1985).

9. Ruth Herschberger, *Adam's Rib* (New York: Harper and

228

Notes and References

Row, 1948).

10. Ruth Hubbard, "Have Only Men Evolved?" In *Women Look at Biology Looking at Women*, Ruth Hubbard, Mary Sue Henifin, and Barbara Fried, eds. (Cambridge: Schenkman Publishing Company, 1979).

11. Sarah Blaffer Hrdy, *The Woman That Never Evolved* (Cambridge: Harvard University Press, 1981).

12. Nancy M. Tanner, *On Becoming Human* (Cambridge, England: Cambridge University Press, 1981).

13. Donna Haraway, *Primate Visions: Gender, Race, and Nature in the World of Modern Science* (New York: Routledge, 1989); see my review of Haraway's book on pp. 187–195 of this collection.

14. Sarah Blaffer Hrdy, "Empathy, Polyandry, and the Myth of the Coy Female." In *Feminist Approaches to Science*, Ruth Bleier, ed. (New York: Pergamon Press, 1986).

15. Ursula M. Franklin, *The Real World of Technology: The 1989 Massey Lectures* (Toronto: CBC Enterprises, 1990).

16. See the set of articles published in the section entitled, "Women's Practices: Another Science?/Les pratiques des femmes: une autre science?" In *Femmes et/Women and Sciences*, Karen Messing, Maria De Koninck, and Lesley Lee, eds. *Resources for Feminist Research*, Vol. 15, No. 3, November 1986.

17. Karen Messing, "Union-initiated Research in Genetic Effects of Workplace Agents." *Genewatch*, Vol. 6, Nos. 4/5, 1990.

Index

Index

232

Index

Index

Index

Index

Index

contribution of, 173
exposure to toxic substances of, 143-144, 173
reproductive investment in, 110
role in fertilization of, 172-174
Steptoe, Patrick, 24
Subjectivity, 120-121, 206-209
Surrogate mothers, 138
Survival of the fittest, 167
Symptoms
  and diseases, 32-33
  severity of, 41

T

Tamoxifen, for breast cancer, 93
Tanner, Nancy, 210
Tay Sachs disease, 62
Technology
  activism and education about, 159-161
  and choice, 155-159
  and Luddites, 153-155
  and profit, 156
  science vs., 163-164
Third World countries, study of non-human primates in, 189-193
Thompson, E. P., 154
Traits
  analogous vs. homologous, 115-117
  genes and, 17-18, 39
  "good" vs. "bad," 23-24
Trefil, James S., 123
Turner syndrome, 174-175
Twin studies, 78-79

U

Ultrasound imaging, of fetus, 55-57, 137-138

W

Walters, Leroy, 28
Wasserman, David, 80
Waste products, 177
Wertz, Dorothy, 44
West, Charles, 107
Western ethnocentrism, 118-119
Whitehead, Alfred North, 65-66
Wilson, Edward O., 87, 108-118, 120, 208
Wilson, Linda, 198
Women
  and AIDS, 94-98
  education of, 103-108
  occupational health of, 99-102
  research on, 96
Women's health, 89-90
Women's health movement, 214-215
Woolf, Virginia, 205
Work-place discrimination, against pregnant women, 142-144

X

X chromosome, 174-175
XYY chromosomal condition, 73, 78

Y

Y chromosome, 174-175
Yeast infections, and AIDS, 96

Z

Zinn, Howard, 182

237

About the Author

Ruth Hubbard grew up in Vienna in the 1920's and 30's. She attended Radcliffe and is professor emerita of biology at Harvard. Hubbard began her career studying physiology and biochemistry and became the first woman to be given a tenured biology professorship at Harvard. She devotes herself to women's studies and social issues in biology. Her essays have appeared in *The New York Times* and she is the author of many books including *The Politics of Women's Biology* and, with her son Elijah Wald, *Exploding the Gene Myth.*